Jerks at Work

How to Deal
With People Problems
and Problem People

By

Ken Lloyd, Ph.D.

Career Press
Franklin Lakes, NJ

JERKS AT WORK
Cover design by Robert Aulcino
Typesetting by Eileen M. Munson
Printed in the U.S.A. by Book-mart Press

To order this title, please call toll-free 1-800-CAREER-1 (NJ and Canada: 201-848-0310) to order using VISA or MasterCard, or for further information on books from Career Press.

The Career Press, Inc., 3 Tice Road, PO Box 687, Franklin Lakes, NJ 07417

Library of Congress Cataloging-in-Publication Data

Lloyd, Kenneth L.
    Jerks at work : how to deal with people problems and problem people / by Kenneth Lloyd.
        p.   cm.
    Includes index.
    ISBN 1-56414-396-1 (pbk.)
    1. Problem employees.   2. Interpersonal relations.   I. Title.
HF5549.5.E42L58   1999
650.1'3--dc21   98-44917

This book is dedicated to

Roberta, Jessica, Stacey, Joshua,
Gaga, and L. K.
Thanks for everything.

Acknowledgments

There are many people who deserve thanks and appreciation for their help in bringing *Jerks at Work* to life. Naturally, there is not a jerk among them.

Over the years that my column has been running in the *Los Angeles Daily News* and several other papers in the United States and Canada, I have received e-mail, letters, and phone calls from readers with all sorts of interesting questions that form the foundation of this book. To these readers, I offer thanks for taking the time to contact me, and I also offer thanks for their confidence in my approach to dealing with people problems and problem people at work. Many of these readers asked me if the columns are available in a book, and their words of encouragement in this area played a key role in my decision to write this book. So, although I write an advice column, I thank my many readers for their advice.

Thanks are due to many people at the *Los Angeles Daily News*, the first paper to run my column. David Butler, the editor, has been a source of solid advice, counsel, and support. Thanks, also, to Chris Parker, the business editor, whose innovative ideas have had such a positive impact throughout the Business section. And, to Minerva Hernandez and the staff, thanks for your help.

There have been several people at Career Press who literally could not have been more helpful and supportive. For all the time, energy, and creativity that they put into this project, I thank publisher Ron Fry, Betsy Sheldon, Eileen Munson, Anne Brooks, Mike Gaffney, and all of the other members of the Career Press team.

Thanks, also, to Gloria Anderson, president of The New York Times Syndicate, and Nancy Beth Jackson, consultant, for their support of my column.

For his advice regarding the most current legal rulings and statutes in the area of employment law, I thank my long-time friend and an outstanding attorney-at-law, Michael L. Stern.

And, finally, I thank my special editor and librarian, Roberta Winston Lloyd, whose insight, understanding, and patience on this project, and on all other projects, know no limits.

Contents

Introduction   9

Chapter 1
Pre-employment Problems   11

Chapter 2
New Employee on the Block   23

Chapter 3
Managers Who Just Don't Get It   39

Chapter 4
Fellow Employees Who Just Don't Get It   65

Chapter 5
Subordinates Who Just Don't Get It   81

Chapter 6
Mismanagement vs. Missing Management   91

Chapter 7
Who's in Charge?   103

Chapter 8
In All Fairness   117

Chapter 9
The Feedback Backlash   127

Chapter 10
With Friends Like This   139

Chapter 11
    Pros and Conflicts   151

Chapter 12
    Complaints, Complaints, Complaints   165

Chapter 13
    Securely Dealing with Insecurity   173

Chapter 14
    We Can't Go On Meeting Like This   183

Chapter 15
    Training in Action vs. Training Inaction   195

Chapter 16
    Dollars, Sense, and Incentives   205

Chapter 17
    All in the Family Business   215

Chapter 18
    Secretarial Mistakes or Mystiques   225

Chapter 19
    Environ-Mental Impacts   235

Conclusion   249

Index   251

Introduction

This book answers real questions, from real people, in real jobs, who work with real jerks. The answers are neither hypothetical nor theoretical, and each takes a direct approach to a broad range of issues associated with working with card-carrying jerks.

The questions were originally mailed, e-mailed, or called in to my weekly advice column, *On the Job*, which runs in the *Los Angeles Daily News* and in several newspapers across the United States and in Canada.

Many readers submitted questions that were centered upon matters that could easily fall under the heading "all in a day's work," such as how to ask for a raise or make a resume look better. But there were far more questions that dealt with the problems created by jerks at work. Question after question focused on jerks as managers, jerks as supervisors, jerks as co-workers, jerks as teammates, jerks in the car pool, jerks as friends, jerks as subordinates.... Each of these categories, along with many others, is addressed in this book.

Jerks can be present in every aspect of work life, from the first contact in the employment process to the last day on the job, and at all points in between. For example, jerks can clearly highlight their presence when conducting job interviews, and in the way they treat new employees. At the same time, there are applicants and new employees who feel compelled to demonstrate that they, too, can act like jerks. With every assignment, task, chore, meeting, project, deadline, objective, and interaction, jerks are always seeking that special opportunity to let everyone know who and what they are.

In leadership positions, jerks can truly come into their glory. They can be invisible, omnipresent, inequitable, intransigent, nasty, unfair, unethical—the list goes on and on. And, interestingly, jerks as subordinates can be just as outrageous, as can jerks as co-workers.

One properly placed jerk at virtually any level of an organization can be linked to a vast array of problems that include leadership ineptitude, widespread unfairness, abysmal teamwork, resistance to change, twisted feedback, conflict escalation, pointless meetings, communication breakdowns, employee stagnation, muddled decision-making, inequitable rewards, staff rebelliousness, and a very uncomfortable environment. And, as the number of jerks increases, so increases the number of problems.

Although there are no automatic or canned solutions for the problems that jerks create, there are some strategies that can help, provided that every problem is analyzed individually, and specific steps are developed to handle each. With a solid strategy in mind, many actions taken by jerks can be stopped and prevented, or at the very least, avoided.

As tough as work is, particularly in light of the long and arduous hours that men and women are now putting into their jobs, work can be turned into sheer torture by the presence of just one jerk. Even sadder is the fact that many organizations and even many departments would rejoice if they only had one jerk.

Each day, employees at all levels of virtually every organization wonder how they are going to deal with the jerks. For this unending flow of questions, there are answers. You will find many of them in this book.

Chapter
—1—

Pre-employment Problems

During the process of screening job applicants, employers have seemingly endless opportunities to act like jerks. And, importantly, so do the applicants.

Employers can ask inappropriate questions, use ridiculous tests, rely on useless data, and generally treat the candidate as an expendable item. This makes absolutely no sense, because countless studies have found that one of the most important factors that determine whether an applicant ultimately accepts or rejects a job offer is the way that he or she was treated during the screening process.

Many of these interviewers seem to ignore the fact that the way that a company treats its job applicants is clear indicator of the way that the company treats people in general. Hence, when a solid applicant is treated poorly, the company loses. And, in a tight labor market, this type of treatment makes even less sense.

In screening strong candidates, there is a point when the company becomes interested in a particular individual. At such a point, the applicant no longer needs to sell himself or herself, while those who are screening for the company must assume more of a sales role. Unfortunately, some of them feel that their only role is one of Grand Inquisitor, and this leads to a situation in which their job interviews are really nothing more than exit interviews.

Screening the employer

Q. I would like to know how an applicant can screen an employer before accepting a position. More specifically, how do you find out if an employer is disrespectful, verbally abusive, overly demanding, and/or has a substance abuse problem? I have worked for several employers with these traits.
K.B.

There are several ways to prevent a job interview from being just a few weeks away from an exit interview. The first is to have all of your senses finely tuned to everything that is going on from the second you walk into a company. What do you see? What do you hear? What is the climate like? When there are abusive employers, the air is often thick with tension.

It is important for an interviewee to regard himself or herself as an interviewer, too. Although you obviously will not gain very much by directly asking if the employer is a dictator, you can certainly ask the kinds of questions that can highlight tyrannical management, such as, "How much turnover has there been in this position?"

Whenever possible, you should talk to present employees and to people who worked with or for the company in the past. In addition, you can learn a great deal about many companies through newspaper and magazine articles, as well as through books, such as those that deal with the best firms in which to work. It can also help to check out what people are saying about a given company by using the Internet.

Employers are constantly raising the standards for potential employees, and it sounds like the time has come for you to do likewise with potential employers.

Check this out

Q. I just went through a job interview and then completed a test that asked me to check boxes that best described the way I would handle various stressful situations. I thought the test was an annoying waste of time, and I'm beginning to wonder about a company that would use it. What do you think?
L.S.

There is some irony associated with a test for stress that can actually be a source of stress. However, before passing judgment or passing on this job possibility, it will be helpful to consider some key points about pre-employment testing.

If this test was randomly thrown into the hiring process because a topsider somewhere in the company heard about it, read about it, or stumbled across it, then you have grounds for concern. Tests today should be job-related, and they should be statistically validated to prove that they are predictive of specific aspects of job performance, and they must do so on a non-discriminatory basis.

In the event you are called back for another interview, you can ask about this. Most progressive companies will gladly give you information about their hiring techniques. And, if your inquiry meets resistance, that can be an important piece of data to factor into your employment decision.

Either way, it is important to note that paper-and-pencil personality tests like the one you described are often easily faked. In many cases, people know how they should react in a stressful situation, and they have no trouble checking a box that describes such behavior, while their actual ability to cope with such situations would knock them out of the box altogether.

Up close and too personal

Q. I recently had a job interview, and before the formal questioning began, the interviewer and I had a little ice-breaking chit-chat. In the process, he asked me a bunch of personal questions, including whether I live with my boyfriend. Once the actual interview started, there were no more personal questions. Does this sound right?
G.D.

This sounds right only if the company is looking for the right way to get itself into some real trouble. All pre-employment inquiries are supposed to be job-related, and there are clear guidelines in this area. The interviewer's little chit-chat could arguably be construed as pre-employment inquiries, and his question about living with your boyfriend was clearly not job-related.

When an interviewer engages in this type of behavior, it is a bad sign on a number of levels. For example, it raises questions about the interviewer's understanding of employment law, his or her awareness of the rights and needs of employees, insight into today's tight labor market conditions, and grasp of what is truly happening in the world of work.

On a broader basis, the interviewer's behavior raises questions about the company itself. When applicants are treated unprofessionally, the professionalism of the whole company is placed in doubt. Applicants who feel they are treated improperly during the interview process typically think twice about accepting employment with the company. This company would be well-advised to think twice about the way its job interviews are being conducted.

The age-old question

Q. Is there any secret to getting a job when you are no longer under 35? I am 59 and have a wealth of skills and experience. However, after some 10 interviews for positions I was very qualified for, I am still unemployed. I know age discrimination is against the law, but employers never say age is the reason for not hiring me. What can you suggest?
L.H.

In today's tight labor market, any rational company would be foolish to pass on an applicant who has a wealth of skills and experience. The first question that your situation raises is whether you are looking at positions or companies that are truly a good match for you. You may be aiming too low, too high, or at targets that you really would not want to hit.

It is important for prospective employers to see that you are focused on the future, and not on the past. Be sure they understand the active steps that you have taken to keep your knowledge current and your skills sharp. If you have taken classes, particularly any that link high-tech applications to your work, be sure to emphasize this.

Because you are able to get interviews, this means that you are passing the screening of your resume and telephone screening. Perhaps something is working against you in the interview. It may be worthwhile to have a friend take you through a practice interview, and for you to do a little more reading in this area.

Remember that the more the interviewers talk, the more they tend to like the applicants, and if there is a job you really want, be very persistent. This is an excellent time for excellent applicants. Just be sure that you are looking at excellent companies.

What you see *isn't* what you get

Q. We interviewed an individual whom we thought was the ideal candidate. His skills were just what we were looking for, and the chemistry seemed great. Now that he has been on board for a few weeks, I think we made a big mistake. He is totally different from the friendly and easy-going person we interviewed. What happened?
T.G.

When you hire a hopeful applicant, only to see him turn into a hopeless employee, any number of problems could have occurred. In the first place, there is no perfect hiring system. Even if you are using the most sophisticated hiring techniques, all you will be doing is improving the probability of making a successful hire. Hiring errors are still going to occur.

This situation also signals that it may be worthwhile to review your hiring system. This can include updating the job description, making sure the interview process is structured and job-related, and using appropriate steps to take references. During the interview, it is not particularly difficult to determine if the applicant has the skills to get the job done, while it is a more complex matter to predict if he or she has the motivation, persistence, and interpersonal skills to do so effectively. The best way to determine this is to develop a very clear picture of this person's work history.

At the same time, it will also be helpful to look at the level of support and guidance that new employees receive in your company. Is it possible that the applicant thought he was joining a friendly and easy-going company, but found something totally different?

Seeing eye to eye

Q. I just interviewed a young man for a job with our company, and he seems to be well-qualified. However, I was bothered by his failure to look me in the eye when he answered a question. I feel that people who do that aren't telling the truth. Some of my employees tell me that I am way off base on this. Are they right?
C.C.

Although you do not see eye to eye with your employees on this matter, they are absolutely right. There is no evidence that people who do not maintain eye contact are lying.

There are all sorts of biases, preconceptions, and stereotypes about people that can prevent an interviewer from getting an accurate picture of a job applicant. If you allow any of them to get in your way, you will significantly decrease your chances of making a successful and equitable hiring decision.

After all, there is no rule that prescribes how much an interviewee is supposed to look into the eyes of the interviewer. Although some how-to books advise applicants to glance occasionally into the interviewer's eyes, and not to stare, the best advice for interviewees is to be themselves, lest they sell a product that they cannot deliver.

At the same time, there is an interesting aspect of eye contact that may be playing a role here. In some cultures, it is considered impolite to look into the eyes of another. This means that you may be looking at another aspect of diversity in the work force. And, as numerous studies have already found, employee diversity is clearly contributing to increases in organizational effectiveness, innovation, and goal attainment.

The best way to approach any job applicant is with an open mind, and your willingness to think further about the issue of eye contact demonstrates that you have one. From this point, you should be pleased to have found an applicant whom you believe is well-qualified. The best step is to meet with him again to further discuss his work history and to ask him some work-sample questions to assess his expertise. If this is a dishonest individual, it will be reflected far more clearly in his career path than in his eyes.

With reference to personal references

Q. It seems to me that it is useless for an employer to insist that job applicants supply personal references rather than employment references. This practice overlooks an applicant's privacy by having to enlist the assistance of friends to secure employment. Why do so many employers do this?
A.D.

Employers who rely solely on personal references while ignoring employment references are actually ignoring several key aspects of the hiring process. Although there are situations in which personal references can play an important and job-related role, such as in positions that call for security clearances, these references are neither necessary nor appropriate in filling many other positions.

One problem is that personal references are virtually guaranteed to be positive. They are often friends or family who have been prepped to say how wonderful the applicant is. This means that personal references are often biased, inaccurate, and invalid. After all, how many rational applicants provide names of people who are going to verbally thrash them? In the hiring process, personal references are about as meaningful as grades given by a student's friends rather than by the teacher.

It is important for an employer to take references, but they should be employment references. Although today's litigious society has caused many companies to do little more than verify employment dates and perhaps general responsibilities, some will provide more job-related information. And, even if a company will do nothing more than verify dates, that is still important data—it is possible that everything an applicant has said may be false. A reference check with a previous employer is a reality check, while a reference check with a friend is little more than a blank check.

If the companies where you are interviewing ask only for personal references, they are making a mistake. If you are hired, you may want to discuss this with management. In the meantime, there is an approach that may help you get hired: Try to include names of friends with whom you have worked on previous jobs. This will not only provide the potential employer with glowing phrases about what a wonderful person you are, it will also corroborate some of your employment records and provide glowing phrases about what a wonderful *employee* you are.

The silent treatment

Q. I just had a strange job interview. There were two interviewers, but one asked all the questions and the other sat there, said nothing, and spent most of the time doing paperwork. I had no idea how to deal with him, so I said nothing to him. Did I make a mistake?
J.W.

The only mistake that was made in this interview was by the interviewers. Many companies today have learned that when it comes to interviewing, there is some truth to the old adage that two heads are better than one. However, when one of the heads is buried in paperwork, the advantage is lost because the interviewee is out of sight—and out of mind.

There are two possible interpretations of the behavior of the uninvolved interviewer. One is that this was an intentional act designed to see how you react. A few companies still use "stress interviews" in which they try to put an applicant into a perplexing situation to see what he or she does. The problem with such interviews is that they lack validity, consistency, and fairness. In addition, they generally annoy the applicants.

The second interpretation is that the actions of the uninvolved interviewer were unintentional and simply highlighted his lack of understanding of the role and importance of the interview process. Perhaps he was told at the last minute to sit in on the interview, but he still had work to complete and figured that he could do a little of each. Unfortunately, this, too, leads to an annoying interview that lacks validity, consistency, and fairness.

Any action that you could have taken to deal with the preoccupied interviewer can be interpreted as a strength or a weakness. For example, if you had addressed him directly and drawn him out of his paperwork, your behavior could be interpreted positively as a sign of confidence and assertiveness, or negatively as a sign of arrogance and aggressiveness. At the same time, by not addressing him, your behavior could be interpreted as signs of perceptiveness and empathy, or as indicators of timidity and weakness.

Rather than wondering if you made a mistake, which you didn't, it makes far more sense for you to remember that the way companies intentionally or unintentionally treat applicants during the interview process provides real insight into the way they treat people in general. Keep this in mind if a job offer somehow surfaces out of that pile of paperwork.

Money talks

Q. I was laid off from a middle-management position, and I suffered a substantial salary decrease. How should I respond when a prospective employer requests pay information with my resume? My salary is irrelevant and nobody else's business, and some experts advise applicants to never discuss salary until an offer is made.
K.B.

When applying for a job, you are a salesperson trying to sell your labor, and the employer is the customer. It is not altogether realistic to expect the customer to make an offer on a product without having an idea of the price.

In a social situation, your salary is irrelevant and nobody else's business, but this is not the case in the employment process. For example, if a position is budgeted for a given pay range, and your pay expectations far exceed what the employer can afford, both you and the employer can waste a great deal of time in the screening process, only to find that there is a major mismatch on an issue that could have been discovered at step one.

At the same time, if you feel that your previous salary levels are preventing you from even being considered for an interview, try letting several days pass before responding to an ad for a position that interests you, and then mail a crisp and concise letter that delineates the highlights of your career, experience, and education, and how they perfectly fit the position, without any mention of salary. The objective is to let the potential employer see that you are a "priceless" applicant. The risk is that some companies will interpret your failure to include salary information as a failure to follow directions, and your resume will be treated accordingly.

Your crisp letter may still get you in the door, but once you reach the interview stage, it would be a mistake to take the position that you will not discuss pay unless an offer is made—that may be the only position you take with the company. It makes more sense to have a realistic idea of what you are worth in the marketplace, pursue appropriate growth-oriented positions, and be willing to honestly and assertively discuss pay with potential employers. If you keep finding that the price for your labor is too low, remember that the best way to upgrade your marketability is to upgrade your education.

Hello...goodbye

Q. I just had a job interview that went very badly. The interviewer seemed to lose interest in me after the first few minutes, and it ended about 20 minutes later. Is there anything that can be done when an interview is not going well?
N.P.

Most people have gone through at least one job interview where they felt like a Hatfield looking for work with the McCoys. Each faces the other and superficially goes through the motions, while silently thinking that they should have never cancelled their dental appointments for this.

Before trying to come up with a salvage operation to deal with a collapsed interview, the first question is why it broke down in the first place. The fact is that the breakdown was caused by one of two factors: you or the interviewer.

If most of your interviews last as long as an elevator ride, it's time to look honestly at yourself. In handling interviews, the key steps are to be well-prepared, listen carefully, and answer the questions clearly and succinctly. A job interview is actually a sales call where you are the marketing department, salesperson, and product all wrapped up in one. Before most sales calls, it is not uncommon for a salesperson to do some rehearsing, and you may want to consider doing the same before your next interview.

At the same time, some interviewers are the cause of the collapsed interviews. There are those who make snap judgments based on anything but the facts, while others lack the training to know what kinds of questions to ask and how to ask them. Perhaps you encountered one of these minor inquisitors.

If an interview is going south and you want it to go north, you have nothing to lose by expressing your feelings to the interviewer. You should be candid yet non-threatening, and then take the opportunity to add some key piece of information about your work experience that was not previously discussed but is particularly relevant for the job.

For many employers, the interview is actually an opportunity to view how the applicant will work on the job. If you want to show that you are a person who acts with confidence, assertiveness, and self-assurance, you should have no reluctance to grab the reins of a runaway interview.

The waiting game

Q. I was an assistant manager for two years, but my position was eliminated. I stayed with the company, and whenever a posting for assistant manager comes up, I apply for it. During the past eight months, I have gone through three lengthy interviews, but in each case another individual got the job. I was told that the company holds me in high regard and I should be patient. Should I keep trying for this position, or am I wasting my time?
F.L.

Although eight months can feel like eight years when you are in a position that sounds like a holding pattern, it may not be long enough to know if you are wasting time, marking time, or if it is quitting time. However, there is a way to find out.

You should meet with your manager to discuss your career plans and objectives in the company, with particular emphasis on the specific steps to take to increase your likelihood of being promoted. It will also be important to agree upon some performance-related goals for you to meet.

As time passes, keep the communication lines open with your manager, and do not be shy about publicizing your achievements, particularly when you meet the agreed-upon goals. If you do this and still find that the company would rather try your patience than try you as an assistant manager again, then perhaps it is time to find a company that will not only hold you in high regard, but in a higher position as well.

When the interview goes flat

Q. I just went through a second interview for a job that I really want, and I don't think the interview went well. There were five interviewers, and one seemed sort of out of it and the rest were cordial enough, but I just have a sinking feeling. For future interviews, is there something to do when an interview seems flat?
W.K.

Before talking about future strategies, why are you turning your most recent job interview into an exit interview? Unless you are very familiar with the interviewers, you have no way of knowing if their behavior was a form of rejection or adoration.

There are countless cases of individuals who wrapped up interviews certain that they landed the job, only to find a thin envelope in their mailbox the next day. And, conversely, there are people who come out of an interview convinced that it went about as well as a prisoner interrogation, only to find an upbeat message from the employer on their voice-mail.

At this point, your best action is to write a follow-up letter to the company that thanks them for the interview and further expresses your interest in the job. If you are ultimately rejected, there are some basic strategies that may help in future interviews, but most are quite obvious. The best advice is to be a good listener, be succinct, be honest, and be yourself. If they reject you under these circumstances, they may be doing you a big favor.

Chapter
—2—

New
Employee on
the Block

It's the first few weeks on the job. First impressions are formed, and every action seems to be under a microscope. A mistake, a slip-up, an error in judgment at this point can cast a permanent pall on any employee. If there were ever a time to act like anything other than a jerk, this is it. And, ironically, this is a time when card-carrying jerks somehow feel compelled to engage in some outrageous behavior.

For those newly hired into leadership positions, there is a broad array of woefully advised actions, such as instantly filling the walls with degrees, diplomas, and awards, immediately evaluating the staff, coming on too strong, trying to make everybody happy, or aligning too closely with the staff. Having new leadership is a major change in the lives of the employees, and they typically approach a new leader with a combination of concern, trepidation, and anxiety. If that new leader quickly demonstrates behaviors that point to respect and trust for the employees, some of the employees' reticence can be reduced, and some of the barriers on the road to a productive working relationship can be knocked down. However, for those new leaders intent on acting like jerks, the road will be very bumpy indeed.

The tendency to start off on the wrong foot is not limited to newly hired leaders. Employees at any job level can also prove that they are capable of acting like jerks. They can do this in many ways, including excessive resistance, playing an overly rousing game of "test the manager," pressuring the new staff, intently living in the past, and aggressively fighting the future.

Some people think that these questionable behaviors will simply pass in time. Unfortunately, such thinking is merely wishful thinking. At the same time, there are specific actions to take at the first sighting of the quirky behaviors.

The resistance movement

Q. I joined this company as a manager about six months ago. A core of employees has been resistant to me and difficult to manage from day one. They have been with the company for a long time, and they definitely have an attitude. What is the best way to deal with them?
D.D.

If these long-term employees have any interest in becoming even longer-term employees, they need to understand the necessity of working with you, not against you. For the past six months, it sounds like you have been rather tolerant in your dealings with them, and this has generated a rather intolerable situation in return.

The best way to approach this challenge is by having frequent contact and two-way communication with this group, and by trying to include their inputs in establishing plans and goals for the department. In addition, these employees should be encouraged to develop their own performance goals that can contribute to those of the department. Let them see that you are willing to provide active guidance and support throughout the process.

There is a related step that is also worth considering. Within this kind of employee grouping, there typically is a leader who plays a major role in determining acceptable behaviors and attitudes. Although it may be difficult for you to sell your ideas to the group, it is relatively easy for this person to do so. You probably already know who this leader is, and the next step is to meet with him or her. Let this person understand your respect for the experience and expertise of the long-term employees, and then set some clear expectations regarding the kind of leadership role that you would like this person to play among the group. This employee should understand the advantages and opportunities associated with playing such a role.

If the employees do not respond to your positive and supportive approach, then it is appropriate for you to implement your back-up style. In a word, the employees should understand that there is a term that describes their resistant behavior perfectly: *insubordination*. Let them know the specific sanctions that will be applied when their behavior contradicts the established rules, standards, and performance expectations.

Long-term employees are an asset to the organization, but if they have an attitude that places them above it, they can easily become a liability.

To the nth degree

Q. The first thing our new manager did was to put all sorts of degrees, certificates, and awards on his office walls. We are a pretty casual company, and some of us are wondering about him already. What does it mean when a manager does this?
S.G.

At this point, you have minimal behavioral data regarding your new manager, so it is difficult to frame any conclusions. The broader and more important issue is that your manager focused his initial attention on the walls rather than on the employees. After all, one of the first steps for new managers to take is to meet with the troops. This does not have to be the very first step, but it should be higher on the things-to-do list than a hammer-and-nail activity.

This means the real questions about him focus on the priority of his actions, rather than on the number of framed documents that he has nailed onto his walls. When managers adorn their walls in this way, it can mean anything. In some cases, walls that are burgeoning with certificates, photos, and degrees can point to questions about the office holder's ego, but they can just as easily point to an achievement-oriented professional who has worked in organizations where this practice is quite common. The fact is that walls overflowing with personal memorabilia can actually indicate low self-esteem or high self-esteem, lack of confidence or strong confidence, self-doubts or steadfast inner strength. In a word, the practice of filling the walls with mounted milestones tells you very little about your new manager.

At this point, the best step for you is to avoid dwelling on this matter. You have a new manager, and it is only normal for you to have heightened interest as to what he is really like. Rather than trying to draw major conclusions from minor behaviors, it makes more sense to let some time pass and see what the major behaviors look like. If you establish an expectation that you are going to have problems with him, the odds are that this is precisely what will happen.

If you want a hint as to the best way to accelerate communication with him, just ask him about one of his framed items. Perhaps the one generalization you can make is that people enjoy talking about anything they place on their walls.

The tough cookie

Q. We hired a new office manager, and she is a tough customer. Ever since she has been on board, there have been lots of accidents, and we never had a problem with this before. I am starting to think she is the cause. Is that possible?
K.D.

When a manager is described as a "tough customer," this is often a code-word for tyrant. And, when tyranny happens, accidents can happen. However, just because her arrival coincided with an increase in accidents does not automatically mean that she caused them.

For example, it is possible that there were just as many accidents in the past, but the employees were not inclined to report them. They may be reporting them now as a way to get back at the new manager, as well as a way to get some time away from her.

At the same time, she may indeed be causing the accidents because of any number of actions that she is taking. For example, perhaps she is pushing the employees beyond the point of fatigue, or she may have rearranged the work environment so that it is easier for employees to smash into things, or perhaps she has raised the level of stress to new heights.

However, there is also the possibility that the accidents have nothing to do with her. In fact, her actions may have led to fewer accidents than would have been the case if she had not been brought on board. At this point, it is very difficult to know.

You should meet with the employees to discuss the accidents, take corrective actions where possible, and implement a more formalized, publicized, and incentivized safety program. Once such steps have been taken, you will get a better idea as to whether it was an accident to hire this manager.

Come on strong

Q. I was just hired into my first managerial position. Many people advised me to start out as a forceful and strong manager because it is always easier to become less strict. I followed this approach, but I'm getting very little cooperation from the employees. How do I turn things around?
C.J.

The idea of charging into a managerial position as the forceful and strong warrior presents a picturesque image of the heroic manager grappling with a beastly organization, conquering it, and then bestowing benevolence upon its members. The problem is that this approach is straight out of Management Mythology, and myth-management is closely akin to mismanagement.

When entering a new organization as a manager, there is no instantly effective prepackaged managerial style. In some cases, the firm and strong approach may be appropriate, or perhaps even essential. For example, if the ship is rapidly sinking, the new captain is not well-advised to spend time getting to know all of the crew individually, setting up some committees, and then meeting to jointly resolve key issues or problems.

At the same time, if you are the new manager over a department that has highly productive, cooperative, and communicative employees, the idea of entering as some sort of managerial power force is going to undercut your effectiveness as well as that of the department. It's no myth that different situations call for different managerial styles.

This means that you should take a few steps back and carefully look over the effectiveness of your department as an operating entity, and take an equally careful look at the productivity, skills, interaction, motivation, and objectives of your employees. By having a clear understanding of the way that the department operates, as well as the way that the people in it operate, you will have a much better chance of managing it successfully.

Unless you have walked into a major crisis, the best steps for you to take now will be to place far more attention on two-way communication and listening, employee inputs and involvement, managing by wandering around, and increased trust and respect in your dealings with the troops. It is important for a new manager to come on strong—but primarily as a strong listener and communicator.

The old enemy is the new boss

Q. I used to like this job, but I just learned that a co-worker whom I can't stand was promoted to supervisor. She's a know-it-all, and I am very upset about having to report to her. Should I start looking for another job?
D.F.

It is far too early for you to be thinking about getting far away. Because your do-worker was just promoted, there are many things that can happen during her sojourn into supervision. For example, it is possible that her need to show everyone how smart she is will diminish because she now has a title. However, it is equally possible that her promotion will tell her that if she can be an even greater know-it-all, she can be promoted to even greater heights. Or, perhaps she will find that supervision is not for her.

The best action for you to take now is to continue to work as effectively and productively as possible. After all, the actual work that you are doing has not yet changed that much, and you should be able to sense the same levels of satisfaction from it.

By dwelling on the expectation that you are going to have problems with your supervisor, you may inadvertently cause them. If you think that your supervisor is a difficult person, you are likely to adjust your behavior and actually bring out some of her more difficult qualities. In a real sense, you may be creating a self-fulfilling prophecy.

If you absolutely must have some preconceived notions about dealings with your new supervisor, try to put them in a positive context. By setting the expectation that you are going to have a productive and successful working relationship with her, you increase your chances of doing so.

Unless your supervisor is something short of borderline-rational, she will be glad to have a positive and productive employee like you on board. After all, during the first few weeks, she will probably be spending most of her time adjusting to the position and dealing with problem employees and problem situations.

Given some time, you will gain a clear idea as to whether this difficult former co-worker has evolved into a difficult supervisor. If this is the case, then you may want to start considering other actions and options both inside and outside the company.

Slow it down

Q. I am a hard-working individual, and I just joined this company a few months ago. Last week, some of the people I work with told me to slow down because I am making them look bad. I can't believe this type of thing still goes on, and I don't know what to do.
H.A.

In the early days of the Industrial Revolution, you would have been described as a "rate buster," an employee who produces more than his or her co-workers deem to be appropriate. Although your fellow employees may be operating in a mindset that is squarely parked in the eighteenth century, I hope the management of your company is focusing more on the *twenty-first* century, because you need to approach your manager on this situation.

The reason for approaching management first is that if you tell your co-workers that you plan to continue at your present pace, you will end up in a state of conflict with them. And if you go along with their wishes and slow down, you will be in a state of conflict with yourself.

In meeting with your manager, it will be important to do more than complain about the situation. You should let the manager know the facts about the situation, and then present your suggestions as to how to resolve it. For example, something about the present incentive system seems to reward individual performance over group performance, and the result is conflict. With this in mind, you could suggest the implementation of some incentives based on the performance of the department as a team.

Either way, when it comes to your own productivity, you have to remain true to yourself. If this is too much for your present company to handle, there are plenty of companies that can handle hard-working, energetic, and motivated employees.

Test the manager

Q. I was recently promoted to sales manager, and my first duty was to hire a salesperson to fill my former position. The person I hired is older and more experienced than I am. His numbers are good, but he is showing signs of being non-responsive and disrespectful, and now I am having the same trouble with some of the other salespeople. How do I handle this? Do I need to get upper management involved?
S.S.

You are in a classical game of "Test the Manager." The only reason to get upper management involved at this point is if you want to tell them that they promoted the wrong person. You have a real opportunity to demonstrate to your employees, upper management, and yourself that you can manage just fine.

Looking first at your new employee, change the evaluative labels, "non-responsive" and "disrespectful," into actual behaviors. How has he acted to merit these tags? If you can only come up with a feeling that he is ignoring you, then it may be time for some introspection on your part to see if there is anything else about him that may be bothering you.

However, if you can come up with a laundry list of behaviors that clearly demonstrate his lack of respect and his non-responsiveness, then it's time for the one thing that most managers spend the bulk of their time doing: communication. Set a meeting with this employee for a brief review of his performance.

You can open the meeting by mentioning your satisfaction with his numbers, while adding that you are concerned about some easy-to-correct behaviors that are currently creating some difficulties. Importantly, keep the discussion targeted on his behaviors, and not on him personally.

Review his questionable actions and let him see the problems that resulted from them. Listen very carefully to his response—you will get a preview as to where he is going. Let him know that you are willing to work with him to help correct things, but you expect him to develop a plan and commit to it. Wrap up the meeting with positive expectations regarding his future performance and success.

This same approach can be applied to the other members of your sales force. Hopefully they will get the message that it is foolish to be testing the person who gives out the grades.

Out of alignment

Q. We promoted a loyal employee into management, but he seems to align himself with his subordinates rather than with the company on every issue that arises. How do we get him to act more like a manager?

C.J.

Although loyalty is an important factor to consider when promoting employees into management, it is equally important to note that pets are loyal but that does not qualify them for management. Part of the problem may be that you placed too much emphasis on loyalty and too little on the real factors that predict managerial success.

If you really want to know if an employee has a decent chance of succeeding in management, look also to see if he or she is already showing any behaviors that are found in successful managers. For example, is this person playing a leadership role in the department? Is the person particularly effective in organizing his or her work and perhaps that of others? Can you rely on this person for clear and accurate communication, whether written or oral?

If your new manager still identifies with his old pals, the next step is to review the amount of guidance, support, and training that he is receiving from you and your management team. It is possible that he is floundering because your company's approach is to toss new managers into the corporate waters and let them sink or swim on their own. If this is the case, he simply swam back to his friends.

It may also be helpful for you to give him a clearer idea of the kinds of behaviors that you expect him to display as a manager. He will need feedback on any of his actions that undercut his managerial effectiveness, as well as specific guidance on how to handle such situations in the future.

If there are key issues where he feels the employees are right and management is wrong, advise him that he is part of the management team and should be discussing such concerns with his fellow managers. He will need to see that your leadership team is receptive and responsive to his ideas and suggestions, and is oriented toward taking swift action when appropriate.

Your objective is to provide him with all of the resources he needs to succeed in management. If he still cannot act like a manager, perhaps there is an understudy who can.

Instant evaluations

Q. I was just hired as a manager, and I was told today that the performance evaluations of several of my employees are due this month. I know practically nothing about their performance. I was thinking of giving them all average ratings, and then make adjustments on their next evaluation. What do you think?
E.G.

Unless you are looking for instant destruction of your credibility as a manager, do not give your employees instant evaluations. If you go with average ratings, your action is very likely to be perceived as unfair, arbitrary, and focused more on the ritual of the evaluation process rather than the goals of the process.

One possible exception exists if your position had been open for some period of time and there was an interim or acting manager. If this person was in place for at least a few months and is still with the company, you should meet with him or her and review the performance, progress, and attainment of goals for each of your employees. This person should work with you throughout each step of the evaluation process.

Another possible exception exists if your company has a highly goal-oriented evaluation system in which all of the employees established clearly defined and measurable goals at the beginning of the evaluation cycle, and then received documented feedback throughout the cycle. If this is the case, you should review the documentation with your manager and ask for his or her help in rating your employees.

Although there are other limited scenarios in which you may reasonably consider providing evaluations to your employees at this point, unless you are absolutely certain that the evaluations will be accurate, it will make more sense for you to be open with your employees and tell them that you do not have enough data to provide useful evaluations. You should then give them a specific date as to when you will conduct the evaluations. During this interim period, be sure to manage by wandering around, communicate frequently with your employees, and provide them with feedback and coaching along the way.

When new managers come on the job, there are all sorts of traps that can instantly and permanently undermine their effectiveness. Do not let yourself get trapped into giving instant evaluations.

Is everybody happy?

Q. I am a manager, and I was just transferred to another branch to replace a manager who was terminated. He was very lenient, and I'm not. I'm already hearing that the employees are not as happy as they used to be. What do you suggest?
R.C.

When it comes to managers, "lenient" is often a code-word for inept. These are the managers who want to be loved by their employees, and they figure that the best way to accomplish this is to let the employees do whatever they want. The department keeps on running, but no one knows if it's coming or going.

When top management spots the problem, one thing that typically ends up going is the manager, while one thing that typically ends up *coming* is a replacement. If the branch was a nine-to-five happy hour before you arrived, it is only natural that the troops are not as happy now, regardless of your managerial style.

At the same time, it is important for you to do a quick management style check. If you have entered the branch with answers to everything, to the point that you even have answers for which there are no conceivable questions, you will encounter tremendous resistance regardless of your predecessor's style. In addition to resistance, you will find a mixture of dissatisfaction, disappointment, and, of course, unhappiness.

Your best approach is to make sure that you have a good deal of two-way communication with the employees. If there are some "quick-fix" problems that you can correct, do so. Let them see that you are a communicative and responsive leader who listens to what they have to say.

As for their happiness, your objective as a manager is not specifically to make the employees happy. At the same time, you can do so without having to turn your branch into an amusement park.

Try to get to know the employees as individuals, and work with them to formulate goals that will meet their needs as well as those of the branch. With appropriate coaching and recognition, you can help your employees be more productive and meet these goals. When this happens, the direct outcome is that they will sense higher levels of achievement, competence, and personal effectiveness. The indirect outcome is that they will also feel happier. And, so will you.

Some strange advice

Q. I have been with my present employer for less than a month. When I was first hired, my manager said that one of the employees in the department is a little strange. I have worked with this person and have had no problems with him, but I keep thinking about what the manager said. How do I deal with this?
P.L.

This is what happens when you work with a strange person. In this case, however, the strange person is your manager.

It makes no sense for a manager to be saying anything negative about the employees in the department. If there is a problem employee, it is your manager's responsibility to take some action to deal with this person. The appropriate action may be coaching, counseling, or disciplining, but it is not name-calling.

By telling you that your fellow employee is a little strange, your manager is altering your expectations about this person's behaviors. This means that you are more likely to think that his actions are strange, even if they are not. And, because you expect some problems to develop, your own actions may actually trigger some strange behaviors on his part.

At this point, you already have one month's data regarding this so-called strange employee's behavior, and you have found nothing about him that waves a red flag. If there were to be some significant eccentricities or oddities, you probably would have seen them already.

This means that you should make a conscious effort to dismiss your manager's description of this individual and continue to work with him in the same way that you work with any other employee. It will also make sense for you to set some positive expectations about your working relationship with him in the future.

The larger problem in your department continues to be your manager. He has demonstrated a lack of managerial understanding and insight by making his original comment to you, and this certainly is not the only area in which his skills are rather thin. This means that you should be prepared for more surprises in the future, some of which could just as easily be directed at you.

When you have a strong manager, you have a real opportunity to observe high-level managerial behavior and learn from it. In your present situation, the best that can be said is that perhaps your manager will learn something from you.

Blasts from the past

Q. I am relatively new on the job, and most of the people I work with have been here for quite a while. The problem is that they constantly refer to stories and experiences from the past, and I am left out of the conversation. I am tired of this, but I don't know what to do about it.
E.W.

What you are seeing is typical clique behavior, but it obviously does not click with you. Part of the problem is that every organization has its history, humor, culture, and even a climate. Some are warm and hospitable, while others can be nothing short of an ice age. It sounds like your company is parked somewhere on the cooler end of the scale.

You are also experiencing the "new-kid-on-the-block" syndrome. At first, everyone can seem distant and unfriendly, but this can change in time, particularly as you get to know the kids individually, rather than in a pack. One approach is for you to try to take some extra time to get to know your fellow employees individually. There will be some who can talk about issues relevant to the present, and who will also be interested in what you have to say.

It is important to remember that there are always leaders in these groups who set the style and standards for the others to follow. If the leader is open, receptive, and responsive to you, the others will more than likely follow suit. This means that it will be helpful for you to try to identify the leader and get to know him or her, so that the next time the group starts to reminisce for the umpteenth time about some inane event, the leader may put on the brakes and try to include you in the conversation.

In the meantime, it may be worthwhile for you to seek out other newer employees and open the communication lines with them. After all, you already have a good deal in common with them.

On a more long-term basis, it will be important for you to remember how you are feeling today, particularly when you ultimately become a longer-term employee and deal with newly hired personnel.

While a company's climate is about as easy to change as the weather, you and some of the other newer employees can start the process of corporate warming.

The all-around problem person

Q. I have been in my position for 15 years, and last year a new person with a very difficult personality was hired. I have complained to my manager that he is not cooperative, not a team player, and sometimes extremely rude. The last time I went to my manager, I was told that this new hire has been complaining about me! My manager suggested that the three of us meet and "talk it out," but I don't think that my manager has the skill to facilitate such a meeting, and I am not the only one having trouble with the new person. What to do?
L.I.

Your situation typically results from one of two scenarios: In scenario number one, you and your co-workers are a friendly, supportive, and cooperative group, and your employer has succeeded in hiring one of those truly impossible people. If this is the case, your manager can try facilitation, arbitration, or even manipulation, but the prognosis is poor.

In scenario number two, you and your co-workers are still friendly, supportive, and cooperative, but you are a clique. When new employees are hired, unless they somehow fit into the mold, they are excluded. They can then become uncooperative and rude, and can complain about you.

Your first step is to honestly answer which scenario fits. Have your actions and those of your fellow employees brought out the new employee's negative behaviors, or are they something he brought on his own?

In terms of what to do, tell your manager that you would like to try to resolve the matter on your own. You and some of your fellow employees should meet with the new hire, openly discuss specific problematic behaviors displayed by both sides, and jointly commit to a strategy to work more productively together. Be sure to let your manager know about the agreement you reach.

If the problems persist, you should discuss them with the new hire, document them, and then have that meeting with your manager. However, this will not be a meeting to clear the air, but rather will be a meeting to clarify standards, expectations, and consequences in light of documented behaviors. If the new hire has distinguished himself as a truly impossible person, it will be truly impossible for your manager to miss it.

Chapter
—3—

Managers Who Just Don't Get It

There are all sorts of managers who just do not get it. They hold the title of manager, but that is often the only thing about them that has anything to do with management.

The truly excellent managers today understand that management requires true people skills. The bottom line in this area can be summarized in two words: respect and trust. If these values are truly in place, a solid system of management can be built from them.

Certainly the more direct and authoritarian approach to management can work faster and may be more productive, but only over the short term. Given a little time, the dictatorial approach gradually destroys the employees' motivation, drive, commitment, and productivity.

The people-oriented approach is often accompanied by words such as building, creating, innovating, and developing. On the other hand, the authoritarian approach is typically accompanied by words such as destroying, undermining, undercutting, and abusing. There is no question as to which is the approach of choice for jerks.

Stop what you're doing

Q. When I'm working on one project, my manager frequently rushes in and tells me to set it aside and start working on another. I am stressed out, behind on everything, and I don't know what to do. A.S.

It is totally normal for you to be experiencing stress in this situation, as one major factor that causes stress is the placement of obstacles in front of your goals. It sounds like your manager has turned your career path into an obstacle course.

Before taking action, it is important to determine the source of this chaos. On the one hand, you may be reporting to a manager who has minimal ability to plan and organize, while the rest of the company functions on a more orderly basis. On the other hand, the real source of the problem may lie somewhere above your manager, and perhaps your manager is being given "drop everything" orders, too.

If the problem is coming from your manager's inability to manage, the best step is to meet with him or her, explain how his or her current style is preventing you and your associates from effectively completing the work, and then suggest some methods to help correct the problem. For example, it may be helpful to have more frequent meetings, even stand-up meetings, just to review project priorities, progress, and expectations.

However, if your manager's behavior is fairly typical of all managerial personnel in the company, from senior levels on down, then you need to face the fact that you are working in a chaotic company. You are not going to change it, and the real question is whether you are going to change or make a change.

Mood swings

Q. Our manager changes her mood countless times during the day, and we never know if she is going to be friendly or nasty. Sometimes she'll stop and talk with us, and other times she won't give us the time of day. This is driving us crazy, and we don't know what to do about it.
A.T.

When managers run hot and cold, it is not uncommon to find that their employees are upset with the work atmosphere. Unfortunately, your chances of changing your manager are about the same as your chances of changing the weather.

In looking at any job, it is important to separate the variables from the constants. The variables are the parts of the job that *can* be changed or adjusted, such as skill levels, work flow, benefits, and the like. On the other hand, the constants are those parts of the job that are cast in stone. And, the fact is that personality traits tend to be rock-solid.

Because there is no way to make your manager more even-tempered, the only change that can occur in this situation will have to come from you. You need to pay less attention to her mood swings, put them in proper perspective, and focus more on the aspects of your job that are sources of satisfaction rather than dissatisfaction.

Another change that you can make is to alter your behavior in response to her mood swings. When she approaches you or you approach her during one of her cold spells, keep your contact to a minimum and avoid asking for anything. You need to store all of your questions and issues until the storm has passed. Then, when your manager is warm and hospitable, open the floodgates and get as much business done as possible.

Let your manager know how much you appreciate the friendly discussions that you have with her, and let her see the tangible and positive results from them. In this way, you are rewarding the behaviors that you would like her to repeat.

In terms of the bigger picture, if your manager's mood swings are interfering with productivity, you should consider approaching senior management, as this is the type of situation that typically causes topsiders to swing into action.

We interrupt this broadcast

Q. My manager constantly interrupts me, finishes my sentences, and fills in words if I hesitate for even a second. He does this to everyone in our department, and it's driving us crazy. Do we dare say anything to him?
M.D.

The great irony about people who interrupt is that they tend to view others as the interruption. Based on your description of your manager, he sounds like a person who lives life in fast-forward, whether it's talking, walking, eating, or working. He may or may not be a manager who is generally receptive to employees' input, and you should look at his past reactions in order to determine whether a discussion about his interruptions could lead to an interruption in your career.

However, there is one major reason for *not* approaching him on this matter: You have virtually no chance of changing him. What you are seeing is a reflection of his personality, and even if your conversation with him is nothing short of inspirational, he is unlikely to emerge as a changed person. His communication style is part of what and who he is.

Instead of meeting with him to discuss his interruptions, it will make more sense for you to deal with the interruptions when they occur. In this way, rather than trying to change his personality, you are trying to change communication on the job. The next time that he interrupts you, tell him something like, "I know you're busy, but it's important that you know about...." By saying that you know he is busy, you cause him to agree at least with something you are saying. The more he nods when you are talking to him, the more receptive he is going to be to your ideas.

Also, in terms of daily dealings with him, remember that people tend to have more trust in those whom they perceive to be like themselves. Because he is a fast-talker, you should also think about accelerating the pace of your speech. In addition, try to be brief, organized, and to-the-point when you communicate with him.

The reality of your job is that he is your manager, and he is not going to change. Remember that much of your job satisfaction is going to come from sensing high levels of achievement, competence, and productivity in carrying out your responsibilities, and this is where your uninterrupted focus should be.

An open door, and nothing more

Q. The owner of our company has an open door-policy, but whenever any of us meet with him, he doesn't listen. He is friendly, but he always has a reason for doing things his way. Is there a way to change this?

D.F.

There is a major difference between an open door and an open mind. For an open-door policy to have any meaning, there needs to be a true exchange of ideas.

It is very nice for the owner of your company to be friendly and accessible, but his apparent unwillingness to listen indicates that he is rather manipulative. He understands that authoritarian managers who want everything done their way often encounter overt resistance and hostility. However, by being friendly and meeting with the employees, he has found that he can still have everything done his way, and the employees are more likely to acquiesce.

It sounds like you are dealing with a paternalistic leader who believes that he knows what is best for you, whether you like it or not. The approach may be friendly, but it is often the classical fist in a velvet glove.

In order to have any chance at having your ideas heard, you need to approach him in a sales mode. This means that you should open the discussion by having him agree with whatever you are saying, even if it is as basic as the weather.

The next step is to focus on a specific problem and the measurable way in which your suggestion will solve it. Be sure to use words such as profit, achievement, goals, and growth, that will appeal to him as an owner.

You should also try to use a style of speech and body language similar to his. The idea is for him to unconsciously sense that the two of you have much in common and he can trust you. If you still find resistance, tell him that you would like to use your approach on a trial basis in tandem with whatever approach is already in place. Emphasize that he can only win by this proposition.

The problem is that you are dealing with a father-knows-best leader, and even if you come up with a better way to do something, it may be met with an open door, but not with open arms.

Barks and bites

Q. There is a job opening in our company and I told my manager that I would like to apply for it. She snapped at me and said that if she thought I was qualified, she would have come to me. What should I do now?
T.E.

The first step is to recognize that you are reporting to a manager whose range of managerial expertise is best measured in millimeters. Even worse, if a manager snaps at an employee who is interested in further growth and advancement, how does she react when an employee actually does something wrong?

Because you are not dealing with a person who practices rational management, your options are rather limited. Nonetheless, if this is a position you really want, and your manager is the gatekeeper, you will need to approach her again, but this time with a more focused strategy.

The best approach is to use a sales mode in making your presentation to her. Let her see the compelling benefits associated with promoting you. Provide her with a clear picture of the skills, experience, training, and aptitudes that make you a solid candidate. In addition, let her know that you plan to build your skills in areas where you may be weak for this position.

It will also be helpful to let her see how she and the company can profit by promoting you. For example: Time and money can be saved by not having to recruit and interview numerous applicants; there is a need for less orientation time; promoting from within improves employee attitudes and morale; there are distinct advantages in promoting a known commodity. In addition, try to subtly let her see that promoting you is an opportunity for her to look good in the eyes of senior management—your promotion will not only demonstrate her ability to save money, it will also demonstrate her ability to develop promotable employees.

Do not just drop into her office to make this presentation. Rather, call her and ask for the best time for the two of you to meet. If she snaps again and refuses to get together she is giving you a clear snapshot of your future under her.

It's too late

Q. I'm an administrative assistant for the owner of a real estate development firm. I am careful about setting up his appointments, but he is always late. Every day I get calls from people waiting for him, and some are not very pleasant. I mentioned the problem to him once, and he just shrugged. What do you suggest?
S.V.

There is a larger issue underlying this untimely problem—you have a boss who shrugs his shoulders when you want to discuss a problem. This type of response tells you a great deal about his philosophy and style. In a word, it does not sound like he is going to be particularly receptive to any of your ideas to get him to his destinations on time. In fact, it does not sound as if he is particularly receptive to any of your ideas, period.

There can be any number of reasons why people are late, and they run the gamut from unintentional to willful. For example, being late for some people is just a matter of being spread too thin. In order to get one thing done, they push something else back, and the result is a delayed arrival. These are the people who literally run late, as they seem to be running all the time.

At the other end of the spectrum, there are people who are intentionally late because of the message it sends. In a word, it is a show of power and confidence. By making others wait, the message is, "My time is more important than yours, and I don't have to wait for anyone." After all, there are not many kings who sit around and wait for their subjects to arrive for a meeting.

In order to change your boss's behavior, you can certainly adjust his calendar to provide him with more time between appointments, and you can give him positive feedback when he arrives at an appointment close to the due date. However, because you are dealing with a person who shrugs off the idea of arriving somewhere on time, the odds are that he will continue to be late, and you will continue to receive unpleasant phone calls and shrugs. Hopefully, your job has enough other pleasantries to more than counterbalance this treatment.

The imperfect perfectionist

Q. Our manager is a perfectionist who is intolerant of even the slightest mistakes. He can dwell on errors for days, and most of us work in constant fear of slipping up. How can we work for someone like this?

M.A.

The irony in your situation is that your manager is the biggest mistake of all. One of the most important managerial roles today is that of coach, and your manager is more of a tormentor than mentor.

For people to grow, mistakes are an inherent part of the process. And, when an error is met with terror, employees ultimately complete only the most narrow and low-risk aspects of their jobs, and soon become totally dissatisfied. Your manager is taking you down this path.

In dealing with him, be sure to have a clear understanding of his expectations on each project, and devote extra effort to being as careful and accurate as possible in your work.

The next time that he is in an approachable mood, you and your associates should meet with him and let him know that your objectives are the same as his, while adding that it can be difficult to meet these objectives because of his reaction to errors. Tell him that you need his help on this problem, and leave it at that. He is the only one who can change his behavior. If you tell him how to act, you will be making a mistake.

Overwhelmed by oversupervision

Q. I am being oversupervised by my manager. It seems that every time I turn around, he is checking up on me. This is distracting and makes me nervous. How do I get it to stop?
J.S.

Although managers today are often advised to practice management by wandering around, it sounds like your manager is into management by snooping around. This points to a real managerial problem: Either your manager has one, or you are one.

The first thing to do is to review your own performance, with a careful look at the quality and quantity of your work. If things are not up to par, you are sending an invitation to your manager to spend some *quantity* time with you.

Step two of the process is to compare your performance with that of your co-workers. You may think that your work is great, but if it is overshadowed by what your co-workers are doing, it's another invitation.

Armed with this information, you are ready to meet with your manager. Depending on the findings of your performance diagnosis, you should use one of two approaches: If you found that your performance is questionable, you will get nowhere by denying or defending it. It makes more sense to level with your manager and tell him that you would like his help in putting together a self-improvement plan. Be sure to include frequent follow-up dates to meet with him to review your performance—this can help send a message that there is no need for constant monitoring.

At the same time, if you found that your performance is rock solid, tell your manager that you appreciate his accessibility, and then ask if there is any particular reason for the mega-monitoring. If something is bothering him, work out a plan to resolve it. And, if there is no particular reason for this monitoring, tell him that both of you can be more productive if he spends less time positioned over your shoulder. If he acts on this suggestion, he will see that you have handed him the greatest gift an employee can give to a manager—time.

Unfortunately, there are some insecure managers who cannot part with their blanket management style. If he is one, that means that his position is not going to change, which means that you should either try to adjust to it or else change positions yourself.

The blame game

Q. When I came to work a few days ago, my manager instantly blamed me for something that I didn't do. Although she apologized later, I still have a bad feeling about the whole incident. What should I do?
C.N.

When it comes to tossing around blame, no one can blame you for still being upset. You were unjustly slammed by your manager, and it's normal for you to be sensing a combination of anger, frustration, and disappointment. Not only are you hurt by having been erroneously blamed, you are equally upset that your manager could have even considered you to be at fault in the first place.

When a manager acts as instant judge and jury, it is not management at all—it is frontier justice within the corporate walls. Your manager had a hunch that you were the culprit, so she winged you. Then she found out she threw the wrong person in jail, so she issued a "sorry, partner" and rode off into the sunset.

The fact is that real management calls for real communication and coaching, particularly in work situations where problems or mistakes are found. When a manager resorts to instant blaming, it is nothing short of instant mismanagement.

You can let some time pass and hope that this whole incident quickly fades away, which it may well do. But it might not, particularly if you feel that too much was left unsaid.

This means that it will make more sense for you to down with your manager and discuss the matter further. After all, the fact that she could blame you at the outset indicates that her perception of your standards and performance differs markedly from yours.

The first thing to do is to thank her for checking out the situation further and for apologizing to you. From there, indicate that you want to clarify a few points so that this type of problem does not occur again. Then paint a fully detailed picture of your performance. Your main objective is to leave her thinking that there could never be a reason for you to be considered, let alone blamed, for the kind of problem that occurred.

Hopefully, she will also get the less obvious message that managers who shoot from the hip typically hit their own feet and end up with sore underlings.

A low rating for berating

Q. My manager can be very pleasant, but when things are not going the way she wants, she yells, screams, and berates us in front of everyone. She reports to the president of the company, and he does the same thing. What do you suggest?

T.Y.

There are many reasons behind your manager's tendency to go Vesuvian with her staff, and you have already identified the main one: The company president is a yeller and screamer. His membership in this elite society signifies to everyone in management that yelling and screaming are acceptable behaviors.

When your company president explodes, not only is he permitting the managers to do likewise, he is also showing them how. Most people learn a great deal about management from their own managers—yours has no doubt learned some of the finer points about outbursts from him.

In many respects, the behaviors that are planted at the top of the organization spread like ground-cover over the other departments. And, if you plant cabbage, you get cabbage.

Your manager's behavior is part of the company's climate. Like the weather, you cannot do much about it. These downpours are built into your manager's style, and there is no reason or incentive for her to change. In fact, your company president may start to wonder about her intensity and commitment if she were to do so.

Nonetheless, there are a few options for you to consider. In the first place, solicit your manager's input when you see problem situations on the horizon. If things go south afterwards, she may be less inclined to ignite because of her early involvement in the matter.

If you still end up in the middle of one of her management monsoons, do not argue. You will have far more impact if you speak softly, slowly, and firmly.

Between the storms, you should approach her and present factual data that show how her outbursts undermine every objective she has established for your department. Your present acquiescence is telling her that she can continue to tear into you and your co-workers. And worse, it may even signal to her that she can turn up the intensity if she feels like it.

Over time, your manager's torrents can erode your self-esteem. She needs to understand that her yelling and screaming at you must stop. If it doesn't stop, perhaps you should go.

Take it or leave

Q. Whenever we discuss a problem with our manager, he tells us that if we are not happy with the way things are going here, we should leave. It's not as if we are always coming to him with problems, and we don't appreciate this treatment. How should we handle this?
A.E.

This kind of reaction is very common from a manager whose total understanding of management can be summarized on the message from a fortune cookie. His view of employees is that they are as relevant as carpeting, and he feels equally comfortable walking on either.

The most effective managers have a great deal of insight into their employees as individuals, and they treat them as key resources who can make major contributions to the organization. Your manager's comments indicate that he has absolutely no comprehension of the value of the people who report to him.

One key point for you to consider is whether his attitude is a reflection of top management thinking, or if he is just a dinosaur wandering around the organization while waiting for extinction. Either way, the fact that he is in management is not a very promising sign.

In fact, he may have fine-tuned his present approach to people because it is just what top management wants and rewards. If that is the case, there is no reason or incentive for him to make any adjustments.

It is also important to recognize that there is virtually nothing you can say to him to change his style or lack of it. The way that he deals with people is a reflection of his personality.

The best action for you to take is to remember that managers like him are as receptive to discussing problems as farmers are to swarms of locusts. As a result, it will be particularly important for you and your fellow employees to try to solve the problems on your own. If you absolutely must approach him with problems, it is just as much of an absolute must to be ready with possible solutions.

Underlying all of this is the fact that your manager has advised you to leave the company if you are not happy. If you find that large numbers of topsiders share his view, then perhaps his advice is worth following.

Timing is everything

Q. I told my manager that I needed some more time for a particular project, but he pushed me to complete it, and it ended up with several errors. How do you deal with a manager who keeps rushing you, and then complains about your mistakes?
P.A.

Before you rush to draw any conclusions, it is important to consider two key possibilities: If you are already operating at full-throttle, and your manager expects you to somehow perform at super-human speed, this is something to discuss with him. If you are not really pushing yourself, however, this is something to discuss with yourself. Hence, the first step is for you to honestly and objectively look at your own productivity and determine if there is anything about it that may be putting your manager into his rush mode.

If you honestly feel that you are exerting full effort, you should discuss the matter with your manager. Let him see the documented amount of time that you put into the project, and let him know how you would have handled the sections that were in error if you had been given the time. One strategy for the future may be for both of you to review each project more thoroughly at the outset, and to establish more points for discussion along the way. It may also help to break some projects into more manageable components and establish benchmarks from there.

A managerial style that rushes employees is not exactly motivational, and it can actually interfere with productivity. With more planning and communication, perhaps you both can avoid the rush.

The put-down

Q. My sales manager and I were meeting with a very important customer. During my manager's long-winded presentation, he left out an important piece of information. When I started to discuss it, he interrupted me and said that if I had been paying attention, I would have heard him cover it. He is wrong. I was annoyed and embarrassed. He does this to everyone. How do you work with this type of manager?
M.P.

There is nothing quite like public humiliation to build employee resentment. Unfortunately, when you have an insecure manager who is never wrong, this type of behavior is standard aggravating procedure. Your manager does not realize that by trying to make you look foolish, he ends up looking like a fool.

Look at the words you used to describe your manager's behaviors, such as "interrupted," "long-winded," and "absolutely wrong." You may have tolerated his antics in the past, but there is a compounding effect in being subjected to frequent abuse, and it sounds like you are reaching the limit.

If you are truly intent on doing something about this, and your co-workers are just as upset as you, then all of you should meet with him. The objective is not to trash his managerial style, but rather to present some specific suggestions as to the ways in which you and your associates can work more productively with him...and without him.

By any other name

Q. Our department manager has nicknames for all of us. They're not derogatory or insulting, they're just annoying. However, none of us want to confront him. Should we just live with them?
E.S.

Your manager has either spent too much time watching *Top Gun*, or he is spending too much time trying to relive his college fraternity days. Either way, he is not spending too much time reading about management.

Nicknames are supposed to create an aura of teamwork and unity. In many cases, they do just that, particularly for children and adolescents.

On the surface, your manager's practice of nicknaming each member of the department appears to be a reflection of his creativity and desire to bring fun to the job. Beneath this facade, he is actually flexing his power over you. As the giver of names, he is demonstrating that he is the parental figure, and you are the children.

There is also a message in the way that a name is given to the employee in the first place. You were probably not called into his office to select your nickname from a list of flattering descriptors. More than likely, the manager unilaterally pinned a label on you. The underlying message is that this is the way that departmental decisions are to be made, and this probably underlies your reluctance to take any action.

However, when there is an issue that is upsetting the entire department, it's definitely time for a meeting with the manager. The best approach is for two or three of you to meet with him, remembering that you are having a discussion, not a confrontation.

In this meeting, you can instantly grab his attention by using words that have a strong emotional charge for managers. Tell him that there is an issue that is interfering with productivity, communication, and satisfaction for all the employees in the department. Then go right to the point: The nicknames are disturbing and distracting the group, and things would work a lot better if they were lost. Unless he is totally lost, he'll get the message.

Stealing credit where credit is due

Q. A major project in our department was put under my direction. I finished it about a month ago, and I just learned that an outside agency is giving us an award for it. The problem is that my department manager is taking all of the credit, and he is sharing none of the recognition with me. What do you suggest I do?
K.D.

The best step would probably be to take away his crayons and enroll him in a remedial course in management. His behavior clearly demonstrates that he lacks an understanding of even the most basic aspects of what it takes to be an effective manager. He definitely fails when it comes to his knowledge of leadership, motivation, teamwork, and incentives.

The most effective managers take great pride in the successes and accomplishments of their employees. They know that building up their employees as individuals will ultimately build a strong departmental team. In addition, if a manager has some award-winning employees, the reality is that the manager has made himself or herself more promotable.

Unfortunately, there are many managers who totally miss this point and feel threatened by the successes of their employees. They feel that every employee success makes them look increasingly replaceable. The irony is that by usurping an employee's accomplishments, rather than ceremonializing them, the manager is then increasing the likelihood of huge departmental problems down the road, which can lead to his being replaced.

The best step for you is to calmly discuss this with your manager. If you have an emotional meeting and tell him how unfair he is, all you will generate is an argument and increased frustration. A better approach is to take him on a brief point-by-point tour of the completed project and show him your inputs at each step. Then tell him that you are upset about being left out of the award process, and ask him how he would feel and what he would do if he were in your position.

His answer, no matter what it is, should give you a great deal of insight into the best short-term and long-term steps for you not only in viewing this matter, but in viewing your entire job.

Speaking of failures

Q. I didn't do a good job on one of my assignments a few months ago. The problem is that every time I speak with my manager, he makes some disparaging remark about it. How do I get him to stop? H.M.

The fact that your manager looks backward rather than forward actually raises questions about his sense of direction. Whether he likes it or not, when an employee fails on a project, so does the manager. In these cases, the manager typically fails to provide the employee with adequate information, feedback, and support during the project.

His current antics are part of a power play to deny his own role in your failure, and to lock the blame on your shoulders. One option is for you to ignore his unkind cuts. They will probably disappear as soon as one of your fellow employees fails, and that seems very likely given your manager's skills.

On a proactive basis, the next time he focuses on the incident, ask if him there is anything else that you need to do regarding that assignment right now. After he says, "Uh, no," tell him in an upbeat yet businesslike way that you are interested in preventing that type of problem in the future. Then ask him when the two of you can get together to review the status of your current projects.

As you build some successes, he will be less likely to dig up memories of failures. However, remember that although he shuns responsibility when employees fail, he is likely to grab the spotlight when they succeed.

Thanks for nothing

Q. My manager is quick to criticize my co-workers and me when we do something wrong, but he never gives us thanks or credit when we do something right. Is there a way to get him to show some appreciation?
R.M.

Most people in managerial positions understand the importance of thanking their employees for a job well-done. In fact, if you ask your manager about this, the odds are that he can give you a mountain of information regarding positive feedback.

However, he can probably give you an even bigger mountain of excuses for his failure to provide such feedback. For example, he may play the money card, "The thanks I give you is your pay-check," or, the baby card, "I didn't think you needed that much attention," or, the fantasy card, "I'll try in the future."

When managers fail to give their employees the thanks they deserve, it is typical to find that they are not getting much recognition from their own managers, who in turn are not getting much recognition from theirs—all the way to the top. The failure to provide adequate positive feedback typically starts at the most senior levels of an organization and thanklessly trickles down level by level.

This means that the most powerful way to change the behavior of your manager is to change the behavior of the topside leaders. Unfortunately, this falls a little short on the likelihood scale.

However, there is a less powerful approach that can work. The key step is for you and your co-workers to provide each other with open and visible thanks whenever appropriate. The obvious benefit of this behavior is that it will give you some of the recognition you desire. The less apparent benefit is that your manager may observe this behavior and perhaps get the idea.

Managers learn a great deal about leadership from their own managers, but they also learn from their subordinates. If you see your manager trying to emulate some of your positive actions, be sure to let him know that you appreciate his efforts. In a word, if he is trying to become the kind of leader who gives his employees thanks and recognition when due, you should be very thankful.

Hyper-management

Q. My manager always seems like she is in a crisis, and everything is an emergency. She rushes around the office, talks extremely fast, jumps from topic to topic, and never gives me much of a chance to say anything. How do I deal with her?

C.E.

Reporting to a manager who is in a perpetual panic is no picnic. Unfortunately, what you are seeing is a reflection of her personality, rather than a reflection of her managerial skills. The latter can be changed, while the former is firmer.

One possible approach is to use pacing, a technique employed by many great salespeople. The next time you meet with her, try to talk as fast as she does, and try to use body language similar to hers. In a word, you want to mirror the full range of her behaviors.

The theory is that people trust others who are similar to them. Once you build trust, you are more likely to be able to influence her. Use lots of statements to which her only response can be, "Yes," and use words that have a powerful emotional charge for her, such as teamwork, excellence, and success.

Once you get her into this agreement mode, gradually slow down. There is a chance that she will slow down with you and, perhaps for a few moments, you can experience something called communication.

The larger problem is that employees with effective managers have a real opportunity to learn, grow, and build skills to advance their careers. With your manager, all of that is gone. If the situation persists for much longer, perhaps you should be gone, too.

The phantom assignment

Q. My supervisor told me that an important report she assigned to me last month is due next week. The problem is that she never assigned it to me. I told her that, and she said I was wrong and if I couldn't complete it, I should have come to her earlier. What should I do now?

M.M.

What you should be doing now is that report. Tell your supervisor that you firmly believe that it was not originally assigned to you, but you are going to do all in your power to complete it. Go over the priorities of your other projects with her so that they do not interfere with this one, see if there is any flexibility in terms of the due date, and then give the report every ounce of energy that you can muster.

Once it is completed, you should then try to figure out what may have caused the mixup. Talk to your fellow employees about the assignments, review any documentation, and see who has been handling any related projects. It does sound like your supervisor may be the problem, because an effective manager would have followed up on an important project several times, rather than waiting until a week before it is due.

Either way, you need to discuss the entire situation with her in order to prevent this kind of problem in the future. If she is generally well-organized, the two of you can chalk up this situation as nothing more than an aberration. However, if this kind of occurrence is rather common, it sounds like you are going to need plenty of chalk in the future.

The nonstop talker

Q. How do you deal with a manager who talks all the time? He thinks he is this great communicator, but he doesn't listen. For me to get a point across, I have to say it at least five times, and I'm starting to feel it's just not worth it. What ideas do you have? R.A.

Communication is one of the most important managerial functions, and one word that does not describe your manager's communication skills is "great." Great communicators are great listeners.

There is no way for you to go into his psyche and reprogram whatever may be causing him to be in constant verbal overload. All you can do is try to alter the way he communicates with you.

During the course of the day, there are probably times when he is less talkative, such as in the early afternoon or late in the day. You should meet with him during one of these quieter periods.

Your approach should be honest and businesslike, and your comments should be descriptive rather than evaluative. That is, rather than saying that he is too talkative or domineering, describe specific situations in which more two-way communication was needed. Be sure he understands the advantages of such communication, including increased productivity, motivation, and departmental effectiveness.

If you see some signs of improved listening, be sure to give him positive feedback. And if he still refuses to listen, it is time for you to listen to what your better judgment is telling you.

None of your business

Q. I passed the office of one of the employees who report to me and noticed that she was speaking with my manager. I stuck my head and asked my manager if everything is okay, and he abruptly told me that this is none of my business. How does this sound to you?
T.J.

It sounds like your manager was short-changed when interpersonal skills were being distributed. There may be a perfectly legitimate reason for your employee to chat in confidence with your manager, but there is no legitimate reason in the world for your manager to treat you like a villainous intruder.

As part of the trend toward flatter organizations, perhaps your company actively encourages employees at all levels to communicate with each other, and your employee was simply taking advantage of this. However, in light of your manager's reaction, you are probably concerned that this employee may have been talking about you.

Because you are going to be wondering about what may be happening here, you should meet with your manager to discuss the situation. Tell him that you were only interested in trying to help in whatever situation may have prompted your employee to meet with him, and you are troubled by his reaction.

The next step is to be quiet and listen carefully to what he says. His reaction should give you an idea as to whether this matter is or is not your business.

Public humiliation

Q. My manager asked me to make a presentation in front of several members of our department plus two members of senior management. I was about 10 minutes into the presentation when my manager interrupted me and said, "Cut to the chase." I sped through the presentation, but I am upset with him and the whole matter. What should I do?
B.R.

It is always impressive when a manager interrupts an employee's presentation with an overused and trite cliché. This is a critical incident that tells you a great idea about your manager's skills and abilities.

An effective manager meets with his or her employees before they make a presentation in order to review the timetable, and, if necessary, the highlights of the presentation. By humiliating you during the presentation, your manager scored very high on the clueless index.

At this point, the best step is for you to meet with him and express your concern over what happened, and to discuss what needs to be done to prevent a repeat performance. Let him know that for future presentations, you believe it would be helpful for the two of you to meet in advance in order to assure a successful outcome.

Whether he realizes it or not, his actions highlighted his inadequacy as a manager. If this critical incident is typical of his performance, he better cut to the managerial chase before senior management cuts him altogether.

Hearing is different from listening

Q. Whenever I meet with my manager, he talks most of the time. I give him ideas and suggestions, and he seems to hear them, but he doesn't acknowledge them. Then later, he comes up with my ideas and thinks they are his. How do I deal with this?
J.M.

It is indeed difficult to get a self-absorbed person to acknowledge that his great ideas may be something he absorbed from someone else.

One indirect step is to use more redundancy when communicating with him. If there is a key idea you want to bring out, try to express it several different ways so that your manager has little choice but to hear it and clearly understand that you are the source.

A more direct approach is for you to present your idea with more fanfare and attention. For example, rather than just interjecting an idea, introduce it with something like, "I have an idea that may work in this situation...." This will break the flow and create a point where he will be more likely to remember how and when a new thought was introduced.

If you are dealing with a confident manager who is not threatened by employees with good ideas, this approach can help build your working relationship with him. However, if your manager's behavior is a facade for an insecure leader, you can still try this approach, while recognizing that your ideas may generate more resistance than receptiveness. In this latter scenario, another good idea is to keep your options open within and beyond the company.

Kidding on the square

Q. I manage a branch, and my regional manager teases me about being out of the building so often. Part of my job is marketing and by definition I have to spend time in the community. I do not like his little comments, and I am concerned that they may be more than kidding. What is the best way to handle this?
H.T.

Your manager sounds like the mother who gave her son two ties for his birthday. He ran upstairs and put one on, and then proudly returned to show her. Her response was, "You didn't like the other tie?" If you spent a great amount of time in your building, your manager would probably tease you about spending too much time in your office, rather than being out marketing.

The best step is to tell your manager that you would like to give him a marketing update. Show him how many hours you are out of the building each week, what you are doing during those hours, and the extent to which your marketing efforts are paying off. You can then ask him if he would like you to spend more or less time in the field, adding that you thought his comments were subtly calling for you to spend more time inside.

By clarifying mutual expectations in this area, you will be certain that your performance is in the acceptable range. And your manager may better understand that it is rather foolish to expect an employee to wear two ties at the same time.

The memo machine

Q. Our manager sends us memos for everything. She refuses to use e-mail because she says we just delete them, and she wants us to have hard copies. It is annoying to receive all these memos, and we don't know how to stop them. Can you suggest anything?
T.S.

When you have a manager who seeks to "memorize" the department, there are a number of points to consider: In the first place, is there anything about past performance indicating that you and your fellow employees may need extra notification and documentation? If this is the case, you can suggest to your manager that you have literally gotten the messages and would like to work with fewer of them, at least on a trial basis.

There may be other factors causing your manager to be memo-driven. Perhaps her own boss uses them in abundance and insists that she do likewise, or there may be broader company standards that call for them. Or her training and experience may have led her to make them a key component of her managerial style. In any of these cases, you can expect the memos to continue to flow.

If the memos are a recent addition to her managerial repertoire, you can meet with her to discuss their role and priority, and to suggest specific situations in which they may not necessary. However, even if downpour of memos remains torrential, you are arguably in better shape than employees who receive minimal communication from their leadership, other than criticism for failing to understand what their manager may have muttered as a passing thought three months ago.

Ill-advised advice

Q. I manage a branch for a company that has some high-level employees who advise us about ways to improve what we do. The problem is that one of these advisers is very powerful, but his advice is worthless. I'm afraid to say anything, but I don't want to do what he says. My manager has taken the company line and says to go along with the adviser. What should I do?
T.C.

This has all the makings of a tragic epic, hurling you into the position of either following orders or facing grave risk by doing what you feel is right. Before taking a Patrick Henry "liberty or death" stance, there are some other options to consider first.

For example, are you absolutely certain that this adviser's advice is downright useless? Even though he may have presented some questionable ideas in the past, have you truly reviewed his latest brainchild?

If his current idea lives down to your expectations, you should think about approaching management again. However, this time when your boss hides under his desk, you should think about going to his boss. Your objective is not to criticize anyone; rather, you can criticize the advice, and then offer what you think is better for the company.

If you find that you are hitting a corporate wall, and you still feel that it is wrong to follow the adviser's advice, you need to step back and take a careful look at the company itself. After all, Patrick Henry also said, "I know no way of judging of the future but by the past."

Dr. Jekyll and Mr. Hyde

Q. Our branch manager is charming when her superiors come to visit, but the rest of the time she is nasty, uncommunicative, and vindictive. I want to talk to top management about her, but I'll be in trouble if she finds out. How do you deal with someone like this?
A.L.

When you report to an individual who learned her management skills from Dr. Jekyll and Mr. Hyde, there are a few factors to consider before taking action. If you have minimal contact with her and you enjoy your work, there may not be a need to do anything. Just work hard, keep your contact with her to a minimum, and focus on the most satisfying aspects of your job.

You also need to honestly determine whether your feelings are shared by many of your fellow employees, or if this is a conflict between you and your manager. If your feelings are shared by others, then several of you should consider meeting with her. She is not likely to take vindictive action against a substantial percentage of her staff.

If your company has a human resources person, you and some of your associates can also consider discussing situation with him or her, or you can write a factual and businesslike letter to senior management. Although it can be anonymous, ideally it should be signed by many of you.

Just because you have an impossible manager does not mean you are in an impossible situation. However, in considering what to do, remember what Benjamin Franklin said at the signing of the Declaration of Independence, "We must all hang together, or assuredly we shall all hang separately."

Chapter
—4—

Fellow Employees Who Just Don't Get It

Fellow employees are not necessarily good fellows at all. There are all sorts of actions that individuals or groups of employees can take to create aggravations, annoyances, and disservices for other co-workers.

It is certainly worthwhile to encourage these associates to bring their behavior more into alignment with the human race, and there are actions that can encourage them to do so. In the broadest sense, the most effective approach is to focus on the specific behaviors, and not on the clueless employee's personality.

Unfortunately, in many cases the disturbing behaviors are indeed reflections of deeper personality traits, and they are not about to change. This means that although it is the jerk who should be doing the changing, it is often his or her fellow employees who make the adjustment to work around this individual.

Depending upon the range and depth of the clueless behavior, there will come a time when a more senior-level person needs to be brought into the loop. Hopefully this will do more than reveal another level of cluelessness.

The spreader of ill will

Q. One of my fellow employees comes to work when she is sick. Although she claims that she just has allergies, it is not long before I catch her so-called allergies and end up missing work. I don't want to catch her colds any more. What is the best way to deal with her?

J.R.

When a fellow employee literally makes you sick, some of the best steps for you to take will be those that move you away from her. This does not mean that you should treat her as an infested outcast, but it does mean that you can be more conscious of keeping some geography between the two of you, even when you work together.

At the same time, there is absolutely nothing wrong with mentioning to her that she seems pretty sick and may fare better at home with some chicken soup. The idea is to indicate that you are concerned about her health, and you are offering a suggestion that may help. As part of this little discussion, there is also nothing wrong with telling her that you really do not want to catch her cold. This may not send her out the door, but it may help send her a message to be more careful around you.

There can be any number of reasons for her to be wedded to her job in sickness and in health. For example, perhaps she has some deep psychological needs that prevent her from missing work no matter how ill she may be. If this is the case, there is nothing you can say or do to convince her that she would be better off by taking some time off. Or, perhaps your company has an incentive program that rewards employees for uninterrupted attendance, and she stands to lose some significant goodies if she misses work.

Regardless, if everyone seems to be catching her "allergies," you should meet with your manager. Your department is experiencing a situation that is interfering with productivity and is often linked to accidents, mistakes, and absenteeism. For most managers, this is nothing to sneeze at. In addition, if your company has an attendance incentive program, you should mention that it might need a second opinion. Healthy companies tend to focus rewards on service, quality, and productivity.

The noisemaker

Q. I work in a professional office where the work groups are separated by five-foot high partitions. Recently a co-worker was transferred to the group next to mine, and she is extremely loud and boisterous, to the point of disrupting the work of everyone around her. I asked my supervisor, who is also her supervisor, to speak to her, but he said I should do it myself. I think this is his responsibility, and I am afraid of causing tension if I talk to her. What should I do?
L.H.

Problems on the job can come just as easily from the volume of co-workers as from the volume of work. When a loudspeaker takes up residence next to you, there are a few steps that can help move the noise from the foreground to the background.

It is apparent that your supervisor does not want to hear about this matter, at least not at this point. You can debate the appropriateness of his response, but many supervisors want their employees to try to solve problems themselves. In addition, your outspoken co-worker may become even more upset if you approach your supervisor rather than approaching her first.

The best step is to meet with this co-worker. Although you indicated that you are afraid of causing tension by doing so, that will only happen if you take a heavy-handed or judgmental approach.

A better approach is to tell her that you need her help. Indicate that although you understand how important it is for her to actively communicate with others, the configuration of the office makes it difficult for you to communicate and complete your work, particularly when everything she says is as loud in your area as hers. In this way, you are putting the blame on the partitions and not on her, and you are subtly indicating that her conversations are not private. Conclude by telling her that you would appreciate any action she could take to help solve this matter.

If her words continue to bounce off your walls, then it is time for you and your co-workers to meet with your supervisor. Give him the facts of the problem as well as some possible solutions. If he still declines to get involved, you may need to take a step up the corporate ladder to get a real hearing.

The ancient historian

Q. There is an employee in another department who I worked with at a different company over five years ago. For some reason, he keeps talking about a few minor problems that I had on that job, and now several people in this company are asking me about them. If I approach this employee, I am concerned about turning this into a bigger issue, and if I say nothing, he's just going to keep on spreading these stories. What should I do?
C.M.

The reason this employee feels compelled to bring up stories about minor problems in your past is that there may be some major problems in his. His real message is less about you, and more about his own insecurity.

If you take no action in this matter, he may become tired of telling the same tales, or he may not. In terms of your fear of turning this into an even bigger issue by approaching him, the determining factor is *how* you approach him. If you go into tirade mode, then you will simply give him more ammunition. However, if you approach him on a firm, assertive, and businesslike basis, you are far more likely to end the problem.

The idea is to meet with him and describe the exact behaviors that you feel are unacceptable. Let him know that his actions are upsetting and annoying, and then tell him that you want him to stop now. It is also worthwhile to let him know the consequences if he persists. At this point, it is a little early to start rattling sabers, but you can say something like, "I hope I don't have to take any further action to deal with this matter." If he does not get the point, your manager should.

The amateur psychologist

Q. One of the people I work with fashions herself as some sort of amateur psychologist. She is constantly applying psychological labels to everything I do. Our work forces us to have frequent contact, and this is really getting in the way. What's the best way to deal with her?

C.N.

On the one hand, you could ignore her comments, but that would mean being labeled as passive-aggressive and in denial; on the other hand, you could express your annoyance with her psychobabble, but then you run the risk of being labeled as frustrated and hostile.

Her tendency to do this is part of her personality, and there is not much you can do about it. The best approach is to keep your interaction with her focused on work-related matters that deal with the content, timing, deadlines, and objectives of your projects. Although your co-worker may then claim that you are in some kind of avoidance, the only thing you should really avoid is unnecessary communication with her.

If you find that her actions are truly interfering with the work that needs to be done, then you should consider discussing the matter with your manager. Employees who waste excessive amounts of time psyching out their co-workers may actually psych themselves right out of a job.

The teasers

Q. I made the final decision to hire a particular person, and several people who work with me thought I was making a big mistake. It turns out they were right, and I had to let this person go in a matter of weeks. Now these same co-workers are constantly teasing me about this, and it's getting real boring. What can I do?

J.T.

One of the truly great management theorists, William Shakespeare, would contend that your fellow employees protest too much. It would not be surprising to find that they have made more than their fair share of questionable hires, and their reaction to your mistake is a way for them to feel better about their inadequacies in this area.

The good news is that if you take no action at all, the matter will pass in time. Your co-workers will either become just as bored with the subject as you are, or someone else will make a mistake and this lovely group will then pounce on him or her. It can also be argued that if you do not make an issue out of this, your co-workers will not sense much gratification from their annoying behavior, and it will taper off.

However, if you want a faster resolution, find the group's informal leader. Although it is all but impossible for you to persuade the group to change their juvenile behavior, this leader can do so almost instantly.

Meet with this person in private and express your feelings in a friendly and assertive style. Spell out the benefits of stopping the teasing, along with possible costs if it continues. Then ask if he or she has ever made a less-than-perfect hiring decision. When you see the nod in agreement, use that moment to indicate that the teasing is getting a little old and it's time for it to stop. People who are nodding typically continue to do so.

Before you totally blame yourself for hiring the wrong person, it is worth noting that your fellow employees' negative attitudes may have contributed to his or her demise. With this in mind, the larger issue is that there are plenty of companies where the employees focus on successes rather than failures. Perhaps your focus should be on one of these companies.

The blame deflector

Q. There is one person I work with who has a knack for shifting the blame from himself to me every time he does something wrong. He is well-liked by management, and if I ever complain, I will look like the bad guy. How do I deal with him?
L.M.

You are talking about a person who has earned a masters degree in business manipulation. This is typically an individual who creates a scenario where all of the topsiders love him, and if you have a problem with him, you must be the problem. The best way to deal with him is from a distance, unless you enjoy being a cobblestone in his career.

If your work situation prevents you from distancing yourself from him, there is something you can do. The first step is to document things more carefully. Write memos to yourself on the work you are doing with this person, and be sure to detail your actions, his actions, and the progress of the project itself.

In the event that he makes a mistake and then slides the blame over to your side of the table, call him on it with facts and figures. Let him see that the facts unequivocally prove that he was the direct cause of the mistake.

Be prepared for him to respond with a song and dance befitting a Broadway musical, with muddled choruses crying for actions that "we" can take. Your best move is to sit quietly. If he can upset you, he will take that to management and build an entirely different case against you. Let him know that although he caused the problem, you are more than willing to work with him to correct it. After all, the objective is still to get the job done correctly.

Once he sees that you possess sharp facts that can pierce his Teflon shield, he will be less likely to point his finger at you when management asks what happened this time. However, he will be ready to point next time, and whenever he works with you in the future. If you want to head him off, let him know that you plan to document projects with him well into the future.

Although manipulators seem destined to manipulate, you are not destined to be their prey.

The media freaks

Q. Many of the employees in my department watch one television program in particular, and they constantly quote lines from it. I don't watch the show, and their constant references to it are very annoying. What do you think?
G.R.

As much as you would like to reprogram what your fellow employees are watching and saying, your choices are limited.

One is to accept your co-workers as they are and stop focusing on this issue. They are going to mouth these lines no matter what you say or do, because they enjoy the show and feel better by reliving the televised moments. It is not as if they are a clique trying to exclude you, since you could presumably tune in and join the dialogue at any time.

A related option is to focus more attention on the job that has to be done. Television lines do not typically lend themselves to most formal work assignments.

You could also seek out other employees in the company whose interests are closer to yours, even if it is just to take a break from your colleagues. Although an obvious option is to watch the show, you have probably done so already and found the commercials to be more appealing than the story.

The bottom line is that the show's lines have become part of the culture of your company. Although cultures do not go into syndication, they can last a long time.

The bragger

Q. A co-worker of mine constantly rushes to our supervisor and brags about everything she does here, even if it's just completing the most menial chore. None of us can stand listening to her. To make matters worse, now our supervisor is telling us how wonderful she is. What should we do?
A.E.

You are actually dealing with two separate problems here: One is the bragger and the other is your receptive supervisor.

A bragger is programmed to brag. You and your co-workers should not think that you can turn her into a paragon of humility. Her need to wax eloquent about herself is coming from some needs that are well beyond anything that you need to be handling on the job.

People who work with braggers often tend to adjust their own behavior, rather than trying to adjust that of the bragger. The most common adjustment is to place the bragging comments in the same category as the background noise from the air conditioner, elevator, or traffic. This keeps the bragger happy, and the rest of the staff sane.

Your supervisor appears to be a living tribute to the advertising adage that if you hear something often enough, you start to believe it. If he actually has the time to listen to her pronouncements and then take even more time to tell you how wonderful she is, there may be some serious questions about his managerial prowess.

Nonetheless, he has given you an important message in return: He is a buyer when it comes to employee announcements about themselves. If you honestly believe that your performance equals or surpasses that of your bragging associate, you should make sure that your supervisor hears your self-advertisements too.

In making your pitch, it is best to avoid any comments about the bragger. Rather, focus on your own measurable successes on the job. This is obviously not something you should do every day, but if your supervisor is going to be using such information to help determine raises and promotions, you should make sure that you are getting enough visibility.

There is no question that promoting yourself plays an important role in getting yourself promoted.

The slug

Q. Our company places us in small groups and then assigns projects. Another employee and I were just grouped together with a third person who never does any work. We are upset that we are going to have to do everything while she does nothing. What should we do about her?
S.J.

There are a few steps that can be very helpful in energizing a corporate slug, but there is a fundamental question to answer first: Why is she still on the payroll? The fact that she is still around does not paint a very attractive picture of management and your company's systems for monitoring and evaluating employee performance or lack of it.

Nonetheless, if you are going to have any chance of turning your slug into a slugger, you will need to take immediate action.

The three of you should sit down and go over the ground rules. This is the time to clarify and agree upon the group's objectives and the specific roles, responsibilities, priorities, and deadlines necessary to meet them.

Unfortunately, if your co-worker is a dedicated slug, such an agreement may not mean much. As a result, an additional step is to put all of this in writing, and then have each member of the group sign the document. The act of signing one's name can increase the likelihood of increased involvement and commitment.

However, sometimes the world-class slug needs an even stronger push. Fortunately, there is an approach that may work, while also helping to update your company's performance appraisal system. The approach is called peer review, and it means that employees' performance is evaluated by their peers as well as by their supervision. You can suggest to management that this is a cutting-edge evaluation method used by many successful companies for group projects, and it is worth implementing at least on a trial basis.

The reaction by management can tip you off as to the possible presence of slugs lurking about at senior levels of the company, too.

The slacker

Q. I am a second-year law student interning at a medium-sized law firm. There are five interns, and four of us are working hard, while one spends half of her time on personal phone calls. What is the best action for me to take?
C.D.

You have a number of options, and they all depend on your working relationship with the "phony" intern. If your work is totally independent of hers and you do not need to rely on her in any way to get it done, the best action is for you to take no action at all. She is not your problem, but she could become one if you get "hung up" on her phone calls. You should simply treat the calls as background noise and ignore them.

However, if this background noise starts to move up in decibels and becomes foreground noise, then you should ask her to tone things down. You would do this whether her conversation dealt with a tennis court date or a municipal court date. As another alternative, if you have a door, this isn't a bad time to see if it works.

On the other hand, if your work is dependent upon hers and she is making it difficult for you to get your job done, then it is time for more definitive action. In such a case, you should communicate directly with her. Let her know precisely what you need, and when you need it. It will be important to focus on the work-related outcomes that you seek, rather than upon her proclivity to spend hours on personal calls.

Many firms that bill by the hour carefully compute staff time and output. It should not take long for management to see that things do not add up for her.

The inn crowd

Q. Several of the people I work with recently started going out after work for some socializing that can take up much of the evening. I have family commitments, so I don't join them. Now it seems that all they talk about is what they did the night before. I don't like it, and I'm not sure what to do.
D.C.

Dealing with a gaggle of fellow employees who have standing reservations on the post-work party barge is never easy. Your feelings are going to be particularly heightened right now because their socializing is a recent phenomenon, which means that the party-pack is still in the infatuation stage where everything is fresh, funny, and exciting.

But, like most other stages, this too shall pass. It is just a matter of time before the happy-hour herd starts to develop some cliques, disagreements, and conflict, all in the context of increasingly repetitious outings. Although these festive federations typically get off to a running start, most either explode, implode, or die of boredom.

In the meantime, your best approach is to continue to do your work as diligently as possible, keeping in mind that your workload demands and responsibilities have not changed as a result of your co-workers' behavior. You still have a job to do, and so do they. Among other things, this means that there is still a need for plenty of communication with them on work-related matters.

You have a unique opportunity to gain a great deal of insight into your fellow employees. They have the choice of banding and bonding with their buddies and totally excluding you, or they can socialize together and still work with you on a friendly, communicative, and businesslike basis—which, coincidentally, is exactly what is delineated in their job descriptions. In terms of present and future working relationships with these co-workers, it is nice to know where you stand when the chips are down, even when the chips are potato chips.

Your letter implies that there are other employees besides yourself who are not socializing after work. Do not overlook them. It would not be surprising to find that you have more in common with them than with the inn crowd.

The meanie

Q. I work with an individual who has a chip on his shoulder. He can go all day and not talk to the four of us who share an office with him. If he does speak to us, it is with an arrogant tone. Is there anything we should say, or just keep ignoring him?
L.R.

The real question is whether your co-worker's chip on his shoulder came from his own head (sort of a chip off the old block), or whether the chip is a result of working with four people who ignore him.

Look first at your group to see if you have formed a clique that makes him an outsider. If this is the case, his behavior may be a defensive reaction to being excluded.

However, if the four of you have honestly tried to communicate with him and include him in the group, only to be ignored or subjected to verbal venom, it is easy to conclude that you should just work around him. However, you have already found that doing so is rather unpleasant.

A different approach is to meet with him and tell him that you need his help. Let him know that you are concerned about working with him, and you would like to know what he needs in order to build a more productive working relationship.

If he picks up the cue, listen carefully to what he says—if he picks up the cue and breaks it, you should go on with your work, recognizing that you did all you could to solve the problem. If his actions are disrupting the productivity of the office, this is a cue that your manager should pick up.

The reporter

Q. What do you do about a co-worker who is constantly reporting to the boss about the poor performance or behavior of the other employees? These "reports" range from exaggerations to outright lies. This person is the boss's buddy, and that makes it very hard for the employees to defend themselves.

P.A.

When a company has this type of buddy system, it points to two main problems: One is your co-worker, and the other is your boss. The first step is for you and your associates to meet with this co-worker and express your dissatisfaction with his or her behavior. Be sure to emphasize that the conversation has nothing to do with the friendship with the boss, and everything to do with spying, lying, and deceit. Tell this person that it is time for the nonsense to stop, adding that you hope you do not have to take further action at a more senior level to get the problem under control.

The next step is for you and your group to meet with this boss. Tell the boss that he or she is being given inaccurate information regarding your performance and behaviors, and then present specific documentation or examples to support your claims. Be sure to indicate that the constant tattling and prattling is undermining the productivity and effectiveness of the group, while adding that if there are negative claims voiced about you or your associates in the future, you would like to discuss the matter.

The weak link in this organizational chain is your boss. If he continues to be enthralled with your co-worker's fictional stories, perhaps it is time to tell the non-fiction version to one of the company's topsiders.

The perfect one

Q. Our company places us in work groups for different projects, and I often end up working with a woman who is never wrong. Everything has to be done her way. I think our manager likes her, but I'm not the only one who has trouble with her. What should I do? I.M.

The first step is to be thankful that you do not report to her. You are not going to change her magnetic personality, and it sounds like you have equally slim chances of convincing management that she either has a problem or is a problem.

This means that the changes in this situation are going to have to come from you. The first step is to tell your manager that you have worked with this person on several occasions and you would like the experience of working with different co-workers.

When you work with this impossible person in the future, keep your contact with her to a minimum and limit your discussion to the tasks at hand. If you find that she is trying to force you and the other team members to meet her goals rather than departmental goals, you and the team should have a little visit with your manager. Do not focus the conversation on this immovable team member, but only on the possibility that the group is being pushed in the wrong direction. The kind of direction that your manager provides will tell you a great deal about where this problem is going.

The vacationists

Q. Three of the people I work with just got back from a vacation that they took together. Now they're constantly talking about this experience, and I am tired of hearing about their adventures. Help! A.B.

Like a bad cold, this will pass in time, although you may be the one that needs to take an aspirin. Your fellow employees are experiencing post-vacation euphoria, and it sounds like they have not yet readjusted their brains to meet the demands of the job.

If you can just hang on for a few weeks, they will become increasingly involved in work responsibilities, while simultaneously becoming bored with retelling the same tales. Naturally, the experiences will stay with them, and their relationships may well be permanently altered. But all of this is currently moving away from the forefront of their minds.

The best thing you can do at this point, assuming you have listened politely to the stories about the low-mileage rental car, the lost luggage, and getting moved from a regular room to a suite for the same price, is to let them talk themselves out. In addition, when you meet with them, try opening the discussion to other matters, such as the work that all of you are supposed to be doing.

The linguists

Q. I am relatively new in this company, and many of the people I work with use a vocabulary that is foreign to me, particularly in terms of made-up words to apply to people or everyday occurrences. I wonder if I just don't fit in here. Is this common?
N.V.

So you do not like sitting around in your cube farm, blame-storming over one issue or another, and feeling like a 404. (Translation: You do not like sitting in your office, discussing work failures, and feeling like you don't know anything.)

There is nothing new about being confused over the words and phrases used by fellow employees. Organizations, like little societies, have always had their own unique vocabularies.

The real problem in your situation is that the company has not done enough to make you feel part of the team. This means that if you want to succeed, you are going to have to act more assertively. If there are words or expressions that you do not understand, ask about them. If using these words makes it easier for you to be understood or get your work done, use them.

In a real sense, you need to try harder to adapt to this new society. The entire process may feel funny or foreign at first, but you will gradually find that you can adjust. In time, you may want to suggest some actions to management that will help facilitate the adjustment of new hires into the company. Unless management is a bunch of 404s, they will take your advice.

Chapter
—5—

Subordinates Who Just Don't Get It

Every manager has had employees who score high on the jerk scale. In this age of increased emphasis on treating employees with respect and trust, it is particularly challenging to do so when encountering employees who demonstrate excessively high levels of arrogance, immaturity, dependence, verbosity, and the like.

You, as a manager, know it is important to know your employees as individuals, particularly in terms of trying to understand their unique drives, needs, and abilities. By doing so, you are in a much better position to productively channel their unique characteristics, as well as to create a work situation in which at least some of the employees' goals align with the organization's goals. Through this approach, you have a far greater likelihood of creating an environment in which the employee will be motivated.

It is interesting to note that several of the problematic characteristics of these employees are actually extensions of what may have been strengths at one point. For example, although arrogance does not play well in most organizations, if it is peeled back just a little, it becomes confidence, a highly valuable characteristic. In this way, badgering becomes inquisitiveness, dependence becomes cooperation, verbosity becomes openness, and the like. It is key for managers to remember that strengths that are pushed to an extreme can become weaknesses, and there are ways to reel in those employees who have stepped over the edge.

Mr. wonderful

Q. We have an employee who is very competent but very arrogant. He does a good job in outside sales, but he has alienated just about everyone who works here. What is the best way to handle this situation?
A.B.

When dealing with employees who may be viewing the world from a pedestal, there are a number of factors to consider before taking action. In the first place, are you absolutely certain that the issue is his arrogance, rather than jealousy by other employees? You have a successful outside salesperson, and it is possible that the employees who are not doing as well may regard his confidence and self-assurance as unbridled arrogance.

If you determine that you are dealing with a certifiably arrogant person, you have some fundamental issues to consider. For example, because he is successfully generating revenue for the company, you may be reluctant to take any action. And further, it is possible that his arrogance plays an important role in his high degree of sales effectiveness. However, remember that he has also shown a high degree of effectiveness in alienating just about all of your employees, and it is safe to predict that his working relationship with them is only going to deteriorate unless some action is taken.

One step is to meet with him and suggest that he do some work in "internal sales." In a word, he needs to market himself better with the other employees. In addition, although you cannot change his personality, you can certainly have an impact on some of his behaviors. Give him specific examples actions that have caused the employees to bristle, and then give him some coaching as to more appropriate actions to take. You can also have him meet with some of your key employees to discuss their working relationship and try jointly develop a strategy to work more productively together.

Because change can be accelerated when people have some incentive for doing so, show him the specific ways that he can be even more successful if he has the support of his fellow employees. After all, the best businesses today have a strong sense of teamwork, unity, and shared purpose. If this is what you want for your business, then this employee needs to understand that you mean business.

The tantrum-thrower

Q. I hired a new manager, and over the past few months, he has lost his temper twice with his employees. His technical skills are strong, but I am very concerned about his temper. How should I deal with this?

B.G.

Because this manager has already lost his temper twice over a period of just a few months, there is one prediction that can be made—he is very likely to lose it again. For whatever reason, he has held onto a behavior that should have been left behind after he passed through the "terrible twos." Unfortunately, it can now make him a terrible manager, too.

If he lacked the skills to perform effectively as a manager, you could find some educational programs and bring him up to speed. However, his temper tantrums are part of his personality, and there is not much you can do to change it. These types of characteristics tend to be quite enduring over the years.

It may be helpful to take a look at the kinds of situations that triggered his explosions and see if there is a way to prevent them. The outbursts more than likely occurred as a result of his subordinates' failure to meet his expectations in some way or another.

This happens to most managers several times a day, but they tend to work on it rather than let it work on them.

The best step for you to take is to advise this manager that his outbursts are not acceptable managerial behavior. You might demonstrate some specific ways to productively handle the kinds of situations that lead to his flare-ups, or suggest that he take a few deep breaths or take a few deep classes. But the fact is that the burden is on him to exert some self-control. Let him know that you have confidence in his ability to do so, and you have positive expectations regarding his future behavior. Finish the discussion by asking him to make a full commitment to you to try to control his temper.

Human behavior sends all kinds of messages, and his actions from this point will tell you a great deal about his suitability for his present position. If he cannot manage the tantrums, he cannot manage.

Analysis paralysis

Q. When I assign work to one particular employee, he tends to over-analyze it and generate tons of data that we don't need. His role is primarily one of researcher, but whenever I tell him that he's going too far, it doesn't seem to have any effect. What do you suggest?
F.J.

As the word implies, research literally means to search again. And, for many people involved in research, there is great joy in searching and searching and searching. It sounds like you definitely have a very joyous employee.

Just as researchers should be spending a great deal of their time researching, managers should be spending a great deal of their time managing. That is the key to handling this situation.

When you assign work to this individual, there will be real problems if you turn him loose and wait to see what he digs up. Rather, the best approach is to initially provide him with a clear understanding of the parameters, focus, benchmarks, and time-tables associated with the work he is expected to complete.

Once he is into the project, it will be important for you to meet with him at various intervals to see how the work is going. At such points, if you find that he has spent too much time poring over an area of seemingly secondary importance, do not play the role of disciplinarian. Rather, play the role of coach and provide him with an explanation as to the steps that he should have taken, along with more focused guidance as to the steps that he should be taking from this point.

Continue to meet with him frequently during the life of the project, on a scheduled as well as informal basis, and provide fine-tuning and direction as needed. And, if you find that he is focusing his research efforts more effectively and productively, give him positive feedback for doing so. When the project is completed, be sure to meet with him and review his overall performance from a coaching perspective.

With all of this in mind, it is equally important to be sure that you are listening carefully to his reasoning for wanting to dig deeper. After all, he is a researcher, and major discoveries do not typically conform to rigid corporate timetables.

The badger

Q. One of the people who reports to me constantly asks me when he is going to get promoted. I don't know when or *if* he is going to get a promotion, and I have told him to stop asking, but he still persists. How do I get him to stop?
G.P.

Your employee is operating under the erroneous assumption that the more you hear his promotional message, the more likely you are to buy it. This constant barrage may sell hamburgers, but it does not sell employees.

In fact, the irony is that his nonstop questions are an indicator that he is probably not ready for promotion. They tell you that he does not have much insight into the impact he has on others, and they raise questions about his communication skills and ability to listen.

Although he earns high scores on the persistence scale, it is important to remember that a strength, when pushed to an extreme, can become a weakness. In his case, persistence has transformed into annoyance.

Although employees are well-advised to let management know they are interested in being promoted, they do not need to do so several times a day. Rather, they should clearly express their interest, particularly during feedback sessions, and then let their performance demonstrate that they are ready.

The next time your employee approaches you with his favorite question, you should simply tell him the truth. You are uncertain as to when a position will open up, you appreciate his interest in being promoted, and you have taken note of it. At the same time, tell him that he is undermining his chances for promotion by his incessant questions.

On a broader basis, it may be helpful for you to consider working with him and with your other employees to create some specific performance development plans that will help them in their current positions and increase their likelihood for personal and career growth in the future.

If he still persists with his questions about being promoted, then it is important to recognize that you are dealing less with the issue of promotion, and more with the issue of an employee who is asking the same question over and over again. And, this is less of a coaching issue and more of a disciplinary issue.

Superbly superstitious

Q. I manage a small department, and one of my employees is very superstitious. She seems to have a superstition for just about everything, and this is getting in the way of her work and the work of the other employees. What's the best way to approach her?
M.E.

When you have an employee who is consumed with superstition, there is an irony because it is rather unlucky for her to be so superstitious. If her rituals were actually bringing her good luck, you would not be trying to figure out what to do with her.

There are very successful businesspeople who have lucky ties, avoid black cats, maneuver around ladders, and no one says much about them. In fact, when they go into their highrise office buildings, there is usually no thirteenth floor.

However, when an employee is engaging in any behavior that is preventing him or her from getting the work done, or if such behaviors are interfering with the work of others, then it is time to address the matter. Because it is unlikely that you will get at whatever is causing your employee to act this way, your best approach is to focus on her specific behaviors.

You should meet with her and indicate that certain aspects of her behavior are interfering with her performance and everyone else's. Be sure to cite some examples, describe better ways to act in such situations, and let her know that you are willing to help. If her work is truly more important than her superstitions, she should hear what you are saying...knock on wood.

Seek the weak

Q. One of the managers who reports to me hires employees whom I regard as marginal. I have suggested that he raise his standards, but I haven't seen any improvement. What should I do from here? W.R.

When it comes to hiring, strong managers hire strong employees, and weak managers hire even weaker employees. In a word, this manager's behavior raises some questions about his effectiveness.

There can be any number of reasons behind his hiring decisions. For example, he may be trolling for bottom-dwellers because he fears that strong employees will make him look weak. Or, perhaps he is hiring marginal employees because he really does not know much about the employee selection process. Either way, it sounds like he needs more than a suggestion to raise his standards.

The first step is to look carefully at his general performance. If his hiring practices are part of a pattern of marginal managerial performance, then it may be time for a more formal evaluation of his work, along with more goal-setting, follow-up, training, and documentation.

At the same time, if he shows strength in most other of management, his questionable hiring techniques may point to little more than a need for additional education and guidance in the selection process itself.

One short-term solution is to work directly with him during the hiring process. Show him how to screen resumes, conduct interviews, and make productive hiring decisions. Over the longer term, if you continue to see marginal hires, be on the lookout for other indicators of marginal performance.

The suggestion boxer

Q. One of the people who reports to me is constantly submitting suggestions that are impossible to implement. In addition, her suggestions have an arrogant tone, almost implying that if I were a decent manager, I would jump at them. I want my employees to come to me with their innovative ideas, but I am really tired of dealing with hers. What's the best way to handle this?
K.E.

When bombarded with unusable suggestions, it is not uncommon to find managers seriously thinking about making a one-word suggestion in reply: Enough! Once the urge to do so passes, there are some productive steps that you can take.

The first is to recognize that the vast majority of employee suggestions are way off the mark. There can be hundreds before a really good one surfaces. If the employees sense that their suggestions are bothersome or burdensome, the flow will drop to a trickle, and there can be a related drop in attitudes and morale as well. The price of being truly receptive to the employee suggestions is wading through an ocean of notions that may be all wet.

It is also important to note that employees are not typically trained in the process of developing and submitting suggestions. As a result, another step that may help is to show them some examples of suggestions that were actually used. This will help reinforce your commitment to implementing employee ideas, and will simultaneously help the employees frame and focus their suggestions before submission.

Another key part of the process is to thank the employees for their suggestions, whether such suggestions are outstanding or outrageous. If a suggestion is unusable, the employee should be provided with an explanation, along with encouragement to try to refine it and continue submitting further suggestions.

The more serious issue is the arrogant tone of your employee's suggestions. The fact is that she is not sending you a suggestion, but is sending you a message instead—she may well be frustrated, dissatisfied, or upset. It will be helpful for you to meet with her to talk more about how things are going on the job.

Because she is so interested in making suggestions, she should be encouraged to develop some that focus on the steps that she can take to increase her job satisfaction, personal growth, and career opportunities.

The commentator

Q. One of my sales reps and I were at a meeting with one of our best customers when this rep made an inappropriate comment that she thought was cute, but it made the customer bristle. I didn't say anything at the time, but I wonder if I did the right thing. And what to do now?

A.F.

It is never a good sign when words like "best customer" and "bristle" are used in the same sentence. At this point, the only way to know if you did the right thing is if your best customer has become your former customer.

There is no precise formula to follow in a sales situation where one of your associates has a judgmental eclipse. Perhaps the best way to determine if you should say something is by looking carefully at your customer's reaction to the comment.

If your customer truly bristled at your colleague's remarks, it may have been helpful for you to try to defuse the situation on the spot. This does not mean that you should have reprimanded your associate in front of the client, unless you wanted to demonstrate that you, too, are capable of incredibly bad judgment. Sometimes a light comment like, "I don't think that came out the way it was intended," followed by an easy apology is all that is necessary. From that point, you can take more direct control of the meeting and keep it focused on business.

In terms of what to do now, there is nothing to discuss with the customer. The incident is over and done. However, your colleague remains an issue. She needs to be given feedback regarding her behavior, as well as guidance regarding professional interaction with customers. She also needs to understand that if she makes any more cute remarks, things will get ugly.

The energizer

Q. One of my employees has been trying to convince me to implement a motivational program that apparently was very successful at a firm similar to ours. I have told him that I do not like the program, but he keeps trying to persuade me. I don't want to be authoritarian, so what do you suggest I do?
G.G.

It is a good sign that one of your employees is motivated to look for ways to improve the company, although it does not sound like he needs much of a motivational program. His actions point to a good deal of loyalty, commitment, and involvement.

Because telling him that you are not interested in the program has not stopped him, there are some other facts that might. In the first place, just because a program was successful at another company does not mean it will have a similar outcome in yours.

In addition, although there was a positive motivational impact after the program was conducted, this does not mean that the program actually caused it. Perhaps there was a pay increase, a change in management, or any other number of changes. The improved motivation was correlated with the program, but was not necessarily caused by it.

And, what is improved motivation anyhow? These programs need to be implemented scientifically and measured against specific standards.

If you are actually looking for this type of program, there are numerous professional firms that can give you all the information you need to make the right decision for your company. And, you should consider including this employee in the decision-making process.

Mismanagement vs. Missing Management

Effective management today relies heavily upon accessibility and responsiveness. Managers at all levels are advised to maintain open-door policies, and it is widely believed that leaders who have a high degree of two-way communication with their employees are able to generate significantly increased levels of satisfaction, commitment, loyalty, and productivity. In fact, one of the most highly touted managerial behaviors is described as "management by wandering around."

At the same time, there are still managers out there who seem to regard Houdini as their mentor, because so many of them know how to disappear. And when managers disappear, bigger problems appear, including dissatisfaction, distrust, confusion, resentment, errors, and the list goes on.

The idea of being a missing manager does not mean that the manager must be physically missing. There are many who are present at work, but for all intents and purposes might as well be on Mars. If they can be pinned down, they fail to listen or respond to the employees in any meaningful way.

Missing managers miss out on countless opportunities, particularly when it comes to building a productive staff, keeping the employees motivated, developing the employees' skills, monitoring progress, and ultimately meeting goals. These managers tend to succeed in one key area: They are quite successful in convincing their employees that they are jerks.

A range of strategies may be useful in these situations, particularly in terms of letting missing managers see that they have actually been remiss as managers.

The brush-off

Q. I am being given the worst assignments. They are the most tedious and boring, and they offer the least opportunity for growth. When I discuss this with my manager, he brushes off my comments and says that all of the work in his department is important, and he tries to match skills with assignments. How should I deal with this?
A.F.

The managerial brush-off is never a good sign. You are approaching your manager with a serious question—and he is responding with platitudes.

However, your first step is to look at yourself to see if you may be the source of the problem. For example, have you developed the skills necessary to complete the assignments that you seek? Or, could it be that your assignments are challenging enough, but you have been through the drill so often that you are bored with them?

If you are truly the recipient of the less-than-desirable assignments, and you honestly believe that you have the skills and abilities to carry out more challenging work, you should meet again with your manager. Rather than expressing dissatisfaction with a particular assignment, ask your manager what you specifically need to do to receive a different type of assignment. The next step is to follow his recommendations and let him know that you are doing so.

If he continues to hand you marginal assignments and platitudes, perhaps it is time to seek out a work situation that truly matches assignments with your skills.

No thanks

Q. I definitely saved my manager on a project that he needed at the eleventh hour. In return, I did not receive so much as a thankyou. I am annoyed but unsure if I should say anything to him. What do you suggest?
W.T.

The first suggestion is to enroll your manager in a class on bonehead management or bonehead manners. There are few excuses for his failure to express appreciation for your work. He may claim that he is overworked, overtired, or overburdened, but perhaps he is over his head.

Before taking any action, you need to be certain that he is aware that you bailed him out. If there is any doubt in his mind, his lack of thanks may indicate nothing more than his lack of knowledge.

If there is no doubt that he knows you saved him, the next question is whether his lack of appreciation is typical of his managerial style. Is he a manager who never uses the words "thank" and "you" in the same sentence, or is he generally responsive in providing employees with credit when due?

Either way, you should discuss the matter with him. However, rather than saying your feelings are hurt, a more effective approach is to ask him if the work you did at the eleventh hour came out all right. If he is a thoughtless manager, at least you will get some positive feedback regarding the outcome of your efforts. And, if you have an enlightened manager who accidentally overlooked giving you kudos, he will take this opportunity to apologize and give thanks.

93

There are many parts of a job that can be rather thankless, but saving your manager from imminent failure should not be one of them.

Don't call us

Q. I just started working as a one-person purchasing department for a company based in another state. My local manager says that the out-of-state office is supposed to provide me with sources to call, but the out-of-state manager says that this is my local manger's responsibility. Furthermore, the company president is supposed to let me know what my commission will be, but he does not return my phone calls. Could you give me some insight on what to do? J.B.

There can be any number of situations in which an employee is failing, but you are in one where the employer is failing. In fact, if an employee did what your employer is doing, that employee would have a good chance of being on the parting side of an exit interview.

Although your local manager and the out-of-state manager are playing a coast-to-coast version of "that's not my job," at least you are in direct contact with the local manager. You should sit down with this individual and assertively present your views on the current mess by giving specific information on what is preventing you from doing your job and expressing your thoughts on the actions that you expect company management to take.

The fact that the company president is playing "dodge-call" with you actually points to two further problems: The first is that the president is sending you a message about the way that you are regarded in the company, as well as a message about the company's management style or lack of it. At this point, even if you reach the president by phone, it is not realistic to think that you are going to have much of an impact on anything through an unwanted call.

The second problem is that you did not obtain a clear statement regarding your commission prior to coming on board. On a broader basis, it sounds like you did not thoroughly check out the job prior to accepting an offer. It is obviously important for company representatives to interview you during the hiring process, but it is equally important for you to interview them. In a word, there should be no surprises for either side once you are hired. Unfortunately, it sounds like you walked into a corporate surprise party.

Although it is remotely possible for you to change this company, if you do not see this happening, perhaps it is time to think about changing companies altogether.

Intermittent management

Q. I am a long-time employee in a customer service department. The problem is that our manager misses an average of one day a week, and this is creating problems for all of us and for the customers. She is a personal friend of the human resources manager, so we can't go there for advice. We are unsure of what to do.
J.R.

When a manager is frequently missing from a department, it is not uncommon to find that the department is frequently missing its objectives, standards, and performance expectations.

The first person to talk to about the case of the missing manager is the manager herself. You should not meet with her alone, but rather with a group of successful employees from your department. If you go one-on-one with her, you will be increasing your vulnerability while decreasing your impact.

In meeting with her, it will be important to avoid any form of personal attack on her dedication, diligence, or sense of responsibility. The best approach is to show her specific instances in which her absence has measurably interfered with the effectiveness of the department. It may also be instructive to show her the way in which these department failures will be visible to senior management.

Many people have a need to help others, and this need should be particularly pronounced for a manager of customer service. With this in mind, tell her that you and the customers need her help in dealing with issues and problems that develop each day on the job. For her to be a real help, she will need to make a commitment to be there.

If your manager still feels that a four-day week is long enough, you should approach the human resources manager, regardless of her friendship with your manager. You should again use the technique of focusing on the facts and soliciting help. If this manager is truly your manager's friend, perhaps she will be more motivated to help her rather than defend her.

However, if your manager persists in believing that each week deserves a holiday, you should consider playing the senior management card. By doing so, you will ultimately find someone in management who understands that your manager's workweek should be made up of the words, "work" and "week."

When opposites don't attract

Q. I am an extrovert, and my manager is introverted, expressionless, and hard to read. This makes it difficult for me to talk to her, and I am not sure how she feels about my work. How can I get a better idea of what she is thinking?
V.A.

Whether you and your manager are introverts, extroverts, or any other kind of "vert" is not the issue here. The fact is that your manager is not providing you with adequate feedback and guidance on your performance, and you are interested in having a better understanding of how you are doing.

Although it is easy enough to infer that you must be doing at least adequately because you are still employed, this hardly qualifies as helpful or motivational feedback. The bottom line is that the communication lines need to be opened, and it looks like you are going to have to take the first step.

Before trying to do so, however, there are a few points to consider. In the first place, your manager's style reflects a combination of factors such as her personality, upbringing, education, values, and culture. If you want to communicate more effectively with her, try to understand these factors and adjust your style accordingly.

Remember that people communicate most effectively with people like themselves.

You indicate that you are an extrovert. If this means that you are fast-talking, volume-enhanced, and hyper-chatty, you may be building more walls than bridges with this manager.

The best way to deal with her is in a calm, reserved, and low-key style. With this style in mind, ask her for a meeting to review your performance. In this meeting, listen to her comments and let her know that you are interested in continuing to grow, develop, and improve your work, and you would like her guidance in helping you do so. You should also indicate that you would like to have this kind of meeting with her on a regular basis.

By taking this approach, you can comfortably open the communication lines with her, receive the feedback you want, and let her know that you are highly motivated to achieve and advance. However, if she will not meet with you, then the issue is really one of incompetence, and you should be thinking about either working around her or looking around for a better opportunity.

Manager in absentia

Q. Our supervisor constantly calls in sick to me or my co-worker. Our department director resigned in May, and no replacement has been hired. Our supervisor should be calling his boss, but he does not want to put his job in jeopardy. This has created a lot of confusion in our department. Please advise us.
T.P.

You are actually facing a twofold problem of mismanagement and missing management. In order to resolve the problem, you need to take action in both of these arenas.

The first place to focus your attention is on your missing supervisor. You should sit down with him and give him the facts regarding the problems that his absences are causing. You can tell him that you are more than willing to assume supervisory responsibilities when he is out, and you appreciate the opportunity to do so. You can even give him some suggestions regarding the kinds of steps that you are willing to take in order to help run things when he is missing.

However, you should add that you and your co-worker are not really trained to run the department, and the real message is that the department needs consistent and professional leadership on a daily basis.

It will be important to tell your supervisor that it would make more sense for him to call his boss whenever he is going to be absent. In addition, you should indicate that you plan to contact his boss if problems develop in the department that you do not know how to handle.

Unfortunately, one of the problems in this scenario may actually be his boss. Because your supervisor is calling you rather than his boss regarding his absences, it sounds like his boss is not up-to-date on your supervisor's attendance. As a result, it is possible that his boss may not be up-to-date on much of anything else that your supervisor is doing. This means that your situation may need to be resolved at an even higher level.

If you meet with your supervisor on this matter, but he still continues to ask you to cover for him because he is going to be absent again, it will be apparent that he is not receptive to your message. Perhaps there is someone up the corporate ladder who is.

Can sell, but canceled

Q. I am a sales rep for a large company, and I work with a senior salesperson. He divided the territory and kept the good accounts for himself while leaving the problems and leftovers for me. We both report to a vice president who cancels every appointment I make with him. I don't want to be branded a troublemaker, but what do I do?
P.J.

The senior salesperson mines all of the gold from your territory and the vice president ignores you, and you are worried about being branded a troublemaker? Frankly, you are the one person who is not a troublemaker.

Troublemakers are people who constantly look for problems rather than solutions. By facing a problem and looking for solutions, you are quite the opposite.

The real problem is that you have bought into the myth that people who stand up for their rights are troublemakers. The fact is that by failing to stand up for your rights, all you've done is make trouble for yourself.

As soon as your territory was dissected, it would have been far more effective for you to take immediate action. In fact, any serious problem at work calls for a serious response. In such a case, you need to decide if your are going to handle the problem or if you are going to let it handle you. By letting some time slide by, it is easy to slip into the role of corporate doormat.

Fortunately, it is not too late to take some action, and it sounds like you do not have much to lose by doing so. Because the senior salesperson is too busy with your best accounts, and the vice president has stamped "canceled" on all scheduled or future meetings with you, it is time to consider a couple of visits.

If the company has a human resources department, you should stop by. However, if this department is not particularly resourceful, you should look up the corporate ladder and visit whoever holds the position over the vice president.

Either way, your approach with these people should not be to blast anybody. The best strategy is to provide them with all the specifics of your situation, and then ask for their advice as to the best way to deal with it.

By looking carefully at their action or inaction, you will have all the advice you need to handle this situation.

Reduced responsibilities

Q. I have been a loyal employee at this company for several years, and I am now a vice president. I have a great deal of expertise that has led to many honors for the company. However, in a recent restructuring, my job responsibilities were grossly reduced. I have tried to talk to the CEO, but he will not return my calls. What do I do now?
A.B.

Topside managers can send a message to the employees by what they say, as well as by what they do not say. When major changes are made to an individual's job, and top management applies corporate camouflage rather than communication, the handwriting has covered the wall.

However, as a long-term senior employee, you owe it to yourself and even to your company to try to have direct contact with the CEO before you consider any further action. The fact that he will not return your phone calls should not deter you. If he will not talk to you by phone, insist on meeting with him. The best corporate leaders can always find time to meet with key employees. If he cannot or will not do so, the message is clear.

In the event that you do have such a meeting, bring the CEO up-to-date as to your department's numerous successes and your strategies and objectives for the future. It is possible that he has been so preoccupied with the big picture that you and your department may have fallen through one of the crevices.

If you do not get this meeting, and the reconfigured job is unacceptable, it's time to network with other professionals in your field. Although there are often too many applicants chasing too few jobs, there are rarely too many excellent applicants. With your significant honors and stable career path, you're far more marketable than you think. Approach the job search in the same way that you would approach a major job project. Set up a detailed plan that includes goals, priorities, strategies, and deadlines—and then work it.

For better or for worse, we are in an era where job loyalty is not highly rewarded. This does not mean that you should not be highly rewarded; it just means that you may have to go elsewhere to get your rewards.

The mythical open door

Q. The top management in our company frequently tells us how available they are, and they place major importance on their open-door policy. I went to senior management concerning a particular problem, and my boss blew up at me for doing this. Did I do something wrong?
J.S.

You took advantage of the company's open-door policy, your manager blew up at you, and you want to know if you did something wrong? What's wrong with this picture?

In the first place, it is unacceptable for your manager to blow up at you, period. And the fact that he did so after you met with senior management leads to two key points: He is not going to be winning any gold medals in management, and, with a manager like this, it is not surprising that you used senior management's open-door policy.

Nonetheless, it is important to note that many companies with open-door policies expect the employees to try to initially resolve concerns by going to their direct supervision, and use the open-door policy only if they are unable to achieve satisfaction at that level. Typically, if you approach senior management with a problem that your own manager can resolve, it is reasonable to expect senior management to hear you out, while suggesting that you deal first with your manager, and then come back to senior management if the issue remains unresolved.

Because you have an exploding manager, senior management may find many employees from your department coming to them rather than to him. If this is indicative of his overall managerial skills, senior management may consider a different open door for him.

Gone but not forgotten

Q. Our manager is out of the building almost all of the time. He says that he is doing public relations and marketing, but we think he is just doing personal business. The question is, should we report this to his boss, or is it none of our business? If he finds out we went to his boss, he could make things very difficult for us.
C.S.

The issue is not whether your manager is doing real business or funny business when he is out of the building, but rather the fact that he is unavailable most of the time, and this is creating problems for you and your associates.

Hence, the first move is to approach your manager during one of his rare appearances and request a departmental meeting. If he agrees to hold one, be sure to use that opportunity to present a clear picture of the problems that his lack of availability is causing, and then ask him if there are any steps that he can take to help this situation. Most managers will get the idea that it makes sense to spend some extra time with the troops.

However, if your manager refuses to hold this meeting, or if he holds it and then remains basically invisible, you should approach senior management. Indicate that you are confused over the extent to which your manager is supposed to be out of the building, and then describe the specific internal problems that are being caused by his unavailability. There may be some compelling reasons for your manager to be out of the building quite often, but, as you suspect, perhaps there are not. Either way, it will be important for management to see that something is missing in this situation.

Chapter
—7—

Who's
in Charge?

A broad range of behaviors by employees at many job levels may point to confusion as to who is really in charge. For example, there are managers who gladly ignore the supervisory personnel who report to them. When these managers want something done, they simply bypass the leaders who report to them and go directly to the staff. Also in this mix, are co-workers who somehow think they are in charge of their peers, along with employees who operate under the misconception that they are in charge of their own managers.

In any of these scenarios, the typical outcome is a combination of confusion, stress, dissatisfaction, and downright aggravation. Many employees who encounter these self-ordained sovereign employees may be quick to describe them as jerks, but they are not quick at all when it comes to dealing with them.

Unless action is taken to counteract these employees, the situation only worsens. Before the feeding frenzy gets totally out of control, there are some steps that may cause these power-ravenous employees to lose their appetites.

Do as I say

Q. My manager has suggested more than a few times that I promote one particular individual to a new position in my department. He says that she seems like an excellent employee, but she is not my first choice. How should I handle this?

J.G.

Much depends on what the word "suggestion" means to your manager. Looking at the history of your working relationship with him, are his suggestions friendly hints or friendly directives?

Your best move is to meet with him to discuss the promotion. Although you can indicate that the employee he spotlighted has some strengths, be sure to present specific data that unequivocally demonstrate that the employee you prefer is better suited for the new position. You should also have an idea of the kind of position that better suits the employee whom your manager prefers.

The fact is that you have continuous performance data on each of the employees in your department, while your manager has bits and pieces of information gathered over time. As a result, you need to fill in the blanks. Be certain that your discussion covers what is best for the company, the department, and the individuals involved. After all, is it fair to his favorite employee to promote her into a position for which she is not qualified?

If your manager still firmly suggests that you promote his choice, it is apparent that he has other reasons for pulling strings for this individual, while simultaneously turning you into a managerial puppet. In such a case, another firm suggestion is for you to keep your options open.

A lesson in undermining

Q. I told my boss that he was not supporting me as a manager. He is the type of person who has to have control, and he keeps people at odds with me so that they have to go to him. I don't see how I can manage a group of people who refuse to listen to me, and then not get supported by my boss when I discuss the problem with him.

J.B.

It is extremely difficult to manage when you are a manager in title only. The fact is that you are entitled to more support.

Although you approached your manager already on this matter and received something less than a sitting ovation, there are still some steps to take. The first is to carefully assess your managerial effectiveness. If there are some employees who will give you honest feedback, you should also approach them.

It will also be helpful for you to meet with your manager again, but not to talk about his lack of support. Rather, ask him to give you specific suggestions regarding the kinds of actions you should take to become a better manager, and ask him for more coaching and guidance as well.

There appears to be a major communication breakdown between you and your manager. The only way to have any chance of repairing it is through more contact with him, but not if such contact is based on complaints. Let your manager see that you are taking active steps to be a better manager. If you still see no support, then it may be time to recognize that in addition to a lack of support, you have irreconcilable differences.

Decision-making vs. decision-faking

Q. The owner of our company is buying another business, and he put me in charge of the existing company. Before he promoted me, every decision was made by him. Even though I've been promoted, people go to him with all their questions and the decision-making still lies with him. I talked with him about this and he said that he should play less of a role, but this is not happening. What do you suggest?

J.B.

When you have been promoted into a position in title only, you are entitled to be annoyed. In order to determine the best steps to take, look at two key players: the owner and yourself.

The first question is whether the owner is truly ready to relinquish some control. As he goes through the process of buying and operating another business, he knows that he should be reducing his role in the existing company, but whether he is capable of doing so is a different matter. It is easy for owners to say they are going to turn the reins over to another leader, but sometimes the reins are actually chains.

You should also look at the skills, experience, and expertise that you bring to a topside managerial position. Are there some clear indicators that demonstrate you are ready to handle this position, such as steadily increasing managerial responsibilities and continuous upgrading of your managerial skills, or are you the likely candidate because of your loyalty and tenure with the company? If your background sounds more like the latter than the former, perhaps the owner unwittingly feels that you are not quite ready for the job.

The next step is to meet with the owner and try to obtain more than a comment from him that he should play less of a role. Present him with a plan that includes objectives, priorities, strategies, and timetables to phase yourself into the managerial position, and to phase him out. You both should review and refine the plan and jointly agree to follow it. It will also be helpful to emphasize your managerial skills and abilities, and seriously consider taking some additional classes in this area. Managerial positions are growing and changing rapidly, and you should let the company owner see that you are doing so as well.

Present company excluded

Q. As a manager myself, I was annoyed to learn that my manager filled an important position under me without including me in the process. When I complained, he told me that I should focus on my main work responsibilities and be thankful for his willingness to take the time to do the hiring. What should I do now?
L.M.

Your manager's behavior is right out of lesson number one in the controlling managers' playbook. The idea is to usurp the employees' major responsibilities, and then label the employees as ingrates if they question such benevolence.

The first step is to meet with the new employee and conduct your own interview. This is not a job interview, but it is similar.

The objective is to discuss this person's work history and gather some insight into his or her experience, expertise, and style. The meeting should include an opportunity for the new hire to question you, along with a discussion of the expectations and standards for the position at hand.

It is easy to have negative feelings toward the new employee because of the way he or she was brought on board, but it's not this individual's fault that your manager played the control card. Remember to keep an open mind in dealing with this person, as you may have an unconscious wish to see a failure just to get back at your manager.

You also need to meet with your manager. Thank him for the time and effort that he put into the hiring process, and indicate that you agree with his comment that you should focus on your main work responsibilities. Then tell him you believe hiring key personnel is one of those responsibilities.

Give him specific information regarding the costs of his current level of involvement in this process, such as the loss of his time, undercutting your authority, and sending a questionable message to the applicant. Give him equally specific information regarding the benefits associated with placing this responsibility in your hands, such as through more productive use of his time, increased likelihood of a successful hire, and a better chance for team-building with the new hire.

Although you cannot change the personality of the controlling manager, you may be able to change his behavior in specific situations by letting him see the costs and benefits associated with his actions.

The end run

Q. I am a department head and my manager has been going around me and dealing directly with my employees. He gives them orders and assignments, and this is upsetting me and them. I asked him to stop, but he has not done so. I am not sure what to do now.
P.A.

The first question for you to address is why your manager feels that it is perfectly acceptable to take a corporate detour around your desk.

In many cases, this type of behavior is an indicator of managerial incompetence. And, this is not just garden-variety incompetence, but something that has far nicer packaging. Side-stepping managers often claim that they engage in this behavior in order to facilitate communication, take faster action on important problems, deal with the troops on a one-on-one basis, and even provide better support to the person being bypassed. Such motives sound lofty, but they are typically voiced by managers who have spent too much of their time reading management books that have more pictures than text.

At the same time, some managers bypass those who report to them if the bypassed individuals are failing to perform satisfactorily. If this is the case, your manager is bypassing you as a short-term solution, and you know what the long-term solution is.

Either way, your next step is to approach him and discuss the situation. Be sure to express yourself with words that have extra significance to him as a manager. Show him specific cases where his behavior actually undermined productivity, communication, coordination, or teamwork, and then emphasize the point that the department will operate more effectively, and he will save a good deal of his own time, if he will deal directly with you, rather than with your troops.

If he still insists on taking a detour around your desk, remember that you can take one around his.

The command performance

Q. One of the people I work with is constantly telling me what to do. She does not have more expertise, and she and I are at the same job level. I have told her that I don't appreciate the orders, but she persists. Is there a better way to deal with her?
W.T.

When dealing with a self-appointed and self-anointed leader, you typically need to do more than say that you don't appreciate the orders. If you want to get through to a co-worker who issues directives, you need a direct approach.

The next time she sends an order, use a businesslike tone and immediately tell her how you feel. Then issue a directive of your own—her orders must cease and desist. Be clear in letting her know that you are not going to follow her orders, and if she keeps dropping them on you, you are going to drop into your manager's office.

If your co-worker senses the slightest possibility that you are going to follow her orders, she will keep issuing them. For example, you can try to ignore the orders, and this may even lead to a temporary reduction in them. But if you then happen to engage in behaviors that look like you are following her orders, she will think you are finally listening to her, and that means more orders.

You are not going to change the personality traits that are causing her to think she is your boss, but by acting assertively, you may be able to change her behavior. However, even that is a tall order, and a meeting with management may still be in order.

Structured autonomy

Q. I am a regional manager, and I am troubled by the performance of one of the branch managers who report to me. When I mentioned this to my manager, he told me to "step back" and let her run the branch. I don't think she's capable of doing so. Do you have any suggestions?
G.P.

When it comes to stepping back and letting managers manage, it sounds like your manager needs to listen more carefully to his own advice. There is a real possibility that he has stepped into your domain and onto your toes.

However, the most appropriate first step is for you to take an honest look at your managerial style and determine whether you are managing or over-managing. If you find that you are making the majority of key decisions, while the branch manager's decisions are limited to issues like the number of keys to duplicate, then it's fairly apparent that your style has gone over the top.

To the extent that the bulk of managerial responsibilities in her branch are now yours, the next question is why. There can typically be one of two answers: Either she is in management meltdown, or you missed the lecture on managerial delegation. If she is in a failure mode, then your actions are appropriate; and, if she is not, then perhaps it is time to loosen the reins.

The broader issue is that your own manager did not discuss the matter with you. Rather, you were simply advised to step back. It would have been far more effective as well as professional for your manager to meet with you and review the overall situation at this branch. However, it is not too late to do so, particularly if you are convinced that you are using the appropriate managerial approach.

You will need to provide your manager with businesslike documentation that demonstrates that your up-close and personal style is essential at this time. If your manager agrees, the next step is for you to continue to coach and guide the branch manager while building the "bench strength" at her branch. However, if your manager still insists that you step back, and he offers no reasonable explanation for doing so, then it's important to recognize that this position may well be a step back in your career.

The order to fire

Q. I am in a management position, and I report to a senior manager. Last week he told me that I am wasting too much time on one particular employee, and he told me to fire her. I believe she is making progress, and I don't want to terminate her. What do you suggest?
C.C.

At various points throughout your career, you will have defining moments, and this is one. You need to decide whether you are a manager or a messenger. If you are truly the manager, it is your job to assess the performance and potential of your employees.

There are all kinds of problems that can develop if you terminate this employee. For example, your credibility as a manager will drop far below zero. Your employees will see that you are not running the department, and this means that they no longer need to listen to you. Because your manager treats you as a corporate doormat, it will not be long before your employees follow suit.

Speaking of suits, this type of termination could lead to a lawsuit. There may be many technicalities involved, but firing the employee under these circumstances may lead to a claim of wrongful termination.

On the other hand, you will be subjecting yourself to possible disciplinary action if you refuse to carry out your manager's directive. In order to avoid this outcome, you should not simply issue a flat refusal. Rather, you should meet with your manager to discuss the matter.

In this meeting, focus initially on your employee's performance, growth, and accomplishments. It will then be helpful to present your plan to help her continue to succeed. As part of this discussion, you should then mention the possible legal liability associated with terminating her as he suggests.

On a broader basis, tell your manager that the department is far more likely to meet its objectives if you have the freedom and autonomy to manage it. Let him know that you appreciate his input regarding the performance of your employees, and it has always been your practice to give all of his input very serious consideration. If he still insists that you follow his directive, it is evident that his definition of manager is different from yours. In reality, this is a defining moment for both of you.

A mettle to meddle

Q. The president of our company founded it roughly 10 years ago. It has grown to be fairly large, and there are clear job titles and an organization chart. The president seems to ignore all of that and meddle into every department. This creates confusion and stress for all of us, but we don't know how to stop him. What do you suggest?
L.B.

It is easier to stop an onrushing hurricane than to stop an onrushing founder whose target is the company's day-to-day operations.

Numerous companies have departments that are left in shambles after the founder has blown through.

Company founders tend to have excellent vision when it comes to matters outside the organization. They can look at an object and see a product, and they can turn almost anyplace into a marketplace. They are most satisfied when working on broad-based projects that call for high levels of creativity.

Getting involved with day-to-day operations is typically not satisfying to company founders at all. In fact, it is often a source of major aggravation for them. Not only do they dislike it, they are not typically very good at it. As insightful as they are when it comes to looking outside the organization, they tend to be that myopic when it comes to looking inside.

That being the case, why are they delving into company operations in the first place? The most common reason is that the company is their baby. They raised it from infancy, and they are having a hard time letting go. Many founders have the underlying feeling that no one can take care of junior as well as they can.

In addition, during a company's early years, founders typically develop a habit of doing a little bit of everything for the company, both inside and out. Most founders later learn that it is easier to break an ironclad contract than break this habit.

If you want to wean the founders from operations, you will need to give them proof that their actions caused some specific problems. In doing so, you should use words that have a strong positive emotional charge for the founders. Demonstrate that their intervention is damaging to productivity, achievement, effectiveness, profit, and growth.

The founder may still blow through your department, but hopefully without the frequency or intensity of a hurricane.

Running off co-workers

Q. We have too much turnover among newly hired staff, and we are convinced that some of the long-term employees are running off the new hires. We have disciplined some employees for their lack of support, but the problem persists. What else should we do?
P.H.

Because the performance of your present employees will not bring them any awards for best supporting actors, there are a number of options to consider. The first step is to review the effectiveness of the company's screening procedures, hiring techniques, orientation, and exit interviews. After all, it may be possible that the new hires are either running themselves off, or are being pushed out by co-workers who question their attitudes, motivation, or commitment.

If you find that the problem is exactly as you described, consider giving some of your present employees, particularly the natural leaders, some mentoring responsibilities with the newly hired staff. Putting the natural leaders in this role will not only help the new employees succeed, it will also help build more overall support for them.

It may also be helpful to conduct some team-building events and programs that bring the newly hired employees and longer-term employees together in informal gatherings as well as in formalized training sessions.

You may also want to provide some recognition and other incentives for increased retention of new employees. However, if the long-termers are willfully running off new employees, it will be important for them to understand that the turnover they cause may be their own.

Going against the group

Q. There is a core of highly skilled employees who report to me but seem to be trying to make me look bad. My manager told me that they met with him, and he said that I should try to pull my department together. I've met with this group and we've had productive discussions, but nothing changes. How do I handle them? E.G.

You are dealing with a cadre of self-inflated employees who believe that their skills provide them with an invincible shield and the right to say and do whatever they want. It is very nice that you have had productive discussions with them, but if you want things to change, it is time to manage them.

If you have evidence that they are trying to make you look bad, isolate the specific behaviors that substantiate this claim, and then call this behavior what it is: insubordination. The next step is to meet with these employees again, only this time you should do so on an individual basis.

Clearly describe the specific inappropriate behavior and let each employee know that it is unacceptable. Give him or her an idea of more suitable alternative behaviors, along with information regarding the consequences associated with continued problems in this area.

These employees are going to push until they find your limit. Let them know they just found it.

Assuming too much

Q. An employee who reports to me has been assuming some of my responsibilities without prior discussion with me and without my approval. She recently made an incorrect decision on a matter that should have been handled by me. I appreciate her desire to do more, but it is creating problems. What's the best way to deal with her?

S.M.

It is appropriate for your employee to take your advice, take your suggestions, or take your guidance, but she should not take your responsibilities. Unless you take some immediate action, she will continue to take more and more of your job.

The first step is to meet with her and clarify what she is supposed to be doing. You can open by telling her that you appreciate and support her desire to grow and assume additional work, but there are some steps that she needs to take prior to doing so. This means that the discussion should focus primarily on the specific functions that she is expected to fulfill, along with the standards, priorities, and deadlines associated with each.

It will be important for her to see the kinds of problems that can develop when she unilaterally assumes responsibilities that are outside of her area of expertise. She should understand that if her workload allows her to take on additional chores, she will need to discuss them with you in advance. You can give her a very simple guideline: When in doubt, check it out.

If you find that she excels at virtually all aspects of her job, you should look for ways to enrich it. For example, are there additional higher-level responsibilities that she can handle? Are there specific classes that you think she should attend? Because her actions may also indicate that she is somewhat dissatisfied with her present job, this may be an opportune time to discuss her long-term career goals, and to work with her in establishing a more formal plan to help her meet them.

If you take these actions and she continues to move into your territory, then you are dealing with a power player. Rather than assuming your responsibilities, the truth is that she is usurping them. She needs to understand that this truth has consequences.

You can't discipline me

Q. I manage a branch in an area where it is very difficult to find job applicants. Because my employees are so hard to replace, I have been reluctant to discipline them for relatively minor infractions. Is this type of flexibility appropriate under the circumstances?
A.F.

The word "flexibility" implies a progressive and responsive managerial style. However, when flexibility is applied to company policy, it often takes on less-flattering definitions, such as inconsistency, unfairness, or arbitrariness.

When management indicates that some rules need not be followed, the employees can hear a much broader message: The rules are written in pencil. This typically causes the employees to develop the attitude that if the policy on one infraction can be ignored, then it can be ignored on others, too.

The ultimate outcome of your flexibility is that you are placing yourself in a no-win situation. If you ignore an infraction, you are setting the stage for even more serious behaviors to be overlooked tomorrow; and if you decide to implement appropriate discipline, claims of favoritism will echo through the halls.

The fact is that many employees feel positive about having the rules enforced because it enhances their sense of safety, security, and equitable treatment. In addition, most employees are not pleased about working with individuals who flaunt the rules. By taking a flexible approach to company policy, you are actually rewarding the rule-breakers and punishing the loyal and dedicated employees.

You are also assuming that enforcing the rules will cause employees to quit. If enforcement means nothing more than dishing out discipline, then turnover may well be the result. However, this need not be the case if you try to approach these employees as a coach, rather than strictly as a judge. Although you would still apply the appropriate disciplinary action, you have a chance of turning some of these employees around by having two-way communication with them, giving them specific information as to better ways to handle the situations that originally got them into trouble, and letting them know that you are ready to help, guide, and support them in their efforts to improve if they can make a commitment to do so.

The bottom line is that company rules should be followed; if they are out-of-date or unrealistic, they should be revised or eliminated. This is the kind of action that flexible managers take.

Chapter
—8—

In
All Fairness

If a company is truly interested in generating some real ill will, one of the best ways to do so is to treat people unfairly. This type of treatment not only causes an employee to become upset with the company, but, if done right, it can cause an employee to become thoroughly annoyed with his or her co-workers, subordinates, work assignments, and virtually every other aspect of the job.

When employees are treated inequitably, it is not uncommon to find that management will proclaim its willingness to look into the situation, or even mention that the problem will be rectified in the future. These lame pronouncements do little more than generate additional annoyance.

When encountering such actions as unfair enforcement of rules, granting some employees the benefits and others the doubts, or throwing bones to the pets and scraps to the rest, employees will consider their leadership to be bona-fide jerks. And this opinion clearly affects their own motivation, loyalty, dedication, commitment, drive, involvement, and performance.

In some organizations, inequitable treatment is practically a tenet in the mission statement, while in others it is more of an outcome than an objective. Either way, it is not something that most employees today are going to quietly accept. In this regard, when faced with unfair treatment, there are some fairly effective steps that can be taken.

Nothing doing

Q. I have a problem handling my frustration and anger over a co-worker who gets away with everything. As a secretarial team, we share responsibilities and managers, but she arrives late, takes an extra 30 minutes for lunch, fudges on her timecard, and is only able to do this because I'm such a good back-up. If I kept her hours, I'd be in trouble, but managers adore and protect her. I've been here 15 years, but I'm thinking about quitting. How can I be happy here?
A.H.

If you and your fellow secretary are in fact a team, you need to call a timeout to meet with her, go over the rules of the game, and let her know the score. You are going to feel much happier just by taking some direct action to deal with this so-called teammate.

Because most people enjoy being able to help others, you should open the conversation by telling her that you need her help. Rather than focusing on generalities, point out the specifics of her behavior that are creating problems for you. For example, avoid saying that it is unfair for her to come to work late, and instead let her see how her behavior is creating more work that you may not be able to complete. Be sure to add that if such work is not finished and management wants to know why, you will have no choice but to tell the truth. Wrap up the conversation by asking her what steps she can take to help correct the problem.

To the extent that she starts to act more like a teammate and less like an opponent, give her appropriate thanks and appreciation. And, if she plays the game her old way, continue to work diligently, while keeping your commitment to give management the facts if your work runs late.

If you do not take any action to deal with her, the frustration you are now experiencing will increase, and this will ultimately interfere with your performance and success. In addition to telling this co-worker the score, you should try to focus more on the aspects of the job that you enjoyed in the past. One of the primary sources of happiness and satisfaction at work comes from sensing a high level of personal productivity.

Exceptions to the rule

Q. In a recent staff meeting, the director of purchasing reminded all of us that if our work hours are 7 a.m. to 4 p.m., we are to keep those hours. We are salaried employees, but were told that regardless of whether we come in an hour earlier to catch up on work, we cannot leave any time before 4 p.m. There are, however, some employees who are "exceptions" to this rule, but the director will not let me move my hours. What do you suggest I do?
S.M.

The director is using a managerial philosophy from *Animal Farm* in which all employees are equal, but some are more equal than others. Unfortunately, when management demands adherence to company rules, and then allows certain "exceptions," it is a sign of other managerial problems, including a lack of trust, respect, and credibility.

It is ironic that management would be rigid about work hours in an era that is typified by increased flexibility. More and more companies are implementing flextime programs and relying on a philosophy that builds jobs around people.

One step is for you and several of your associates to meet with the director and your supervisor regarding the work hours. This is not a complaint session, but rather a constructive discussion in which you suggest an experiment with a flextime program. Be prepared to discuss the program's benefits, the specifics of how it will work, and how you will measure its success. Flextime can truly help a company's effectiveness, and so can flexible management.

A matter of gender

Q. Our manager denigrates the female employees in our department and speaks condescendingly to the women, while openly favoring and promoting the male employees. He also verbally harasses the females. Isn't this a good case for a class-action discrimination lawsuit?
S.C.

It sounds like you are reporting to a graduate of the clueless school of management. Any manager today who engages in these types of behaviors is asking for increases in dissatisfaction, errors, absenteeism, and turnover, along with decreases in productivity, loyalty, teamwork, and commitment.

Although his behavior sounds like it is begging for a lawsuit, the criteria as to what makes a good case for a class-action discrimination lawsuit are complex and best determined by an attorney. Either way, it may be helpful in the short-term for you and your associates to approach the manager to express and document your dissatisfaction with his specific actions. You should also discuss the matter with your company's human resources person if there is one, and meet with senior management, as well.

Let management know about the specifics of the situation, any actions you have already taken, your suggestions and expectations regarding the matter, and the judicious steps you will take if things are not resolved immediately. It is time for management to be clued-in rather than clueless.

Smitten by a flake

Q. Our boss is enamored with an employee who we think is a flake. She is lazy, unorganized, and sloppy. We do not like all the attention that he gives her, and our fear is that she is going to be promoted. What should we do?
G.K.

Most bosses do not scour their departments in the hope of finding a flake that they can promote. In a word, is this person a bona-fide flake, or is it possible that you and your co-workers are a little jealous of an employee who seems to be getting excessive attention?

Assuming that your perceptions are accurate and this co-worker seems to have stepped right out of a cereal box, the next step is to try to figure out why your boss is so fond of her. For example, could she be performing well in one or two areas that are particularly important to the boss? Although she may generally be a sloth, perhaps she can handle a few seemingly lesser responsibilities extremely well. If that is the case, take a look at your performance in those areas.

At the same time, if you can find absolutely nothing redeeming about her work, then it appears that your boss is letting factors unrelated to performance influence his opinion of her. The fact that you used the word "enamored" in describing his feelings toward her is quite telling.

If he is truly smitten with this employee, your best move is to focus on your own performance and productivity, and make sure that your boss has a clear understanding of your effectiveness and accomplishments. And if he continues to dote over her and even promotes her, then your best move is to another department or beyond.

How fair are you?

Q. I have tried to be a very fair manager, and I became distressed when one of my employees told me that she thinks I play favorites. I told her that I don't, but I would keep her comments in mind. In the meantime, I'm not sure what else to do.
M.J.

High-level managers show high levels of favoritism all the time, and this is entirely proper. The fact is that they tend to favor employees who are productive, industrious, persistent, and committed to high quality.

The problems arise when favoritism is based on factors unrelated to job performance, such as race, gender, religion, or national origin. Your first step is to look honestly at the kind of favoritism you are showing. If it is based on non-work factors, then you should take your employee's comments to heart before she takes you to court.

However, if your favoritism is based on performance, you should inform your employee of this fact, and then give her some advice as to the kinds of actions that can help her become more productive. This may include attending classes, refocusing job priorities, and more frequent communication with you. By giving her additional guidance in this area, you will be doing her a favor, and doing yourself a favor, as well.

At the top of the nitpick list

> Q. My manager is always nitpicking my work and making critical comments about it. I work very hard, but it never seems to be good enough for her. She is nowhere near this tough on the other employees, and they have even said this to me. I don't want special treatment; I'm just tired of being singled out for criticism. What should I do?
>
> E.J.

When you are under the managerial microscope, it is typically either a good sign or something close to an exit sign. On the one hand, your manager may have high expectations of you and is willing to devote extra effort toward critiquing and improving your performance. On the other hand, your manager may be rather exasperated with your performance and may be setting the stage for a change to be made.

The first step is for you to honestly appraise your own performance. Look carefully at the accuracy of the feedback your manager has given you. If she is way off the mark, the best approach is for you to present her with clear, accurate, and irrefutable facts on a calm and businesslike basis.

At the same time, if there is even a hint of accuracy in her critical comments, the only way to lessen such criticism is through a change in your performance. The best approach is for you to have a high degree of contact and communication with her while you are working on your projects. Get a clear understanding of what you are supposed to do at the outset, and then meet with her several times along the way in order to be certain that all of the nits have been picked.

It will also be helpful for you to do some public relations regarding your performance. If there are situations in which you can implement some of her inputs, do so and let her know about it.

To the extent that your manager senses that you are listening to her, respecting her judgment, utilizing some of her suggestions, and arguably upgrading your performance, she will be less likely to be so critical of what you are doing. However, if she still keeps giving you two thumbs down, then it is time for you to consider meeting with her manager to provide your own review of her performance.

The favored one returns

Q. I am in sales and I like my job. Until a few weeks ago, I was given at least eight good leads per week. Then the salesperson who had my territory before me was hired back. My manager said that this salesperson would be given a small part of my territory and none of my leads, but now my leads have dropped to a trickle, and my manager said he will not discuss this with me. What should I do? S.H.

Although your manager is playing the incommunicado card, the only way to deal with this matter is to deal directly with him. The fact is that he unilaterally cut your territory and your leads. These are very unkind cuts.

As a successful salesperson, you undoubtedly have the persistence and persuasive skills to deal with an uncommunicative customer. In such a case, you would probably try any number of strategies to reopen the lines of communication, and that is just what you should do now.

Call your manager again, but do not ask if the two of you can meet; rather, all you want to know is the best time to get together. If you have this meeting, you should express your thoughts about what is going on in your territory, and then jointly discuss the ways in which you can work most productively, successfully, and profitably for the company. Pay careful attention because your manager will communicate something very important about your career with the company, whether he meets with you or not.

The dumping ground

Q. Whenever there are unpleasant assignments, they are given to me. I don't think this is fair, and I don't know what to do about it. C.G.

There is a range of reasons why the less-than-desirable chores seem to consistently wind up in the hands of one person. Looking at the positive side of the range, you are being given this work because management knows that you are the one person who can get it done. And, importantly, you do not complain.

Looking at the negative side of the range, this work is falling in your lap because management recognizes the unpleasantness of these tasks and for some reason feels that you deserve this grief. And, once again, you do not complain.

Your first step is to try to find your position on this range. If you are somewhere toward the positive end, you should feel pretty good. Management views you as a reliable achiever who can effectively handle the less desirable work, which also means that you may well be targeted for promotion.

However, if you are somewhere toward the negative end, you may want to think about acting more assertively. It is possible you are viewed as the corporate dumping ground. Rather than targeting you for promotion, management views you as a target.

At the same time, management does not turn an employee into a victim. Rather, the employee allows himself or herself to be victimized. When you sit silently and absorb outrageous assignments, your behavior is actually calling for more of the same.

If you want the nasty assignments to stop, you will need to approach management and follow a businesslike yet assertive track: Describe the problem in specific job-related terms, voice your feelings about the matter, and then present your thoughts regarding the kinds of actions that need to be taken. If you do not want to be a victim, the first step is to avoid acting like one.

By acting assertively, you demonstrate confidence, self-reliance, and independence, all of which are factors that management seeks in employees who are candidates for promotion. The unpleasant chores may still flow your way, but by acting assertively, you become less of a victim and more of an achiever.

In the spotlight

Q. It's very apparent to everyone that our manager shows favoritism toward me. Although I have no problem with this, the issue is that my friends are giving me a bad time about it. How do I handle them?
R.C.

At some point or another during a career, in addition to having 15 minutes of fame, every employee will have fleeting minutes of favoritism. Your time has arrived, but it does not come without some baggage.

The more that your manager pours praise and perks upon you, the more that your friends will bristle. When it comes to friendship, remember that friends cry when you fail, and they cry when you succeed, but for very different reasons.

The reality is that you are now face-to-face with their very green jealousy. Teasing you is a way for them to vent their frustration while building their own sense of power and camaraderie.

There are a number of ways to deal with friends when this happens. Some employees in your position consciously or unwittingly engage in a form of "dumbing down" so that they will gradually fall out of favor with the manager and then be reaccepted by the group. Unless your peers are more important than your career, this is a step to avoid.

You could sit down with your friends and express your disappointment in their behavior, but there is no reason to think that a guilt launch is going to have much of an impact. If you do take this approach, be prepared to hear comments pointing to how much you have changed and how different you are now.

By showing that you are upset with their comments, you are actually rewarding your friends because that is the reaction they are seeking. A better approach is to continue to be friendly and businesslike, while totally ignoring their petty comments. By doing this, you take all the fun and satisfaction out of badgering you. And, when the behavior ceases to be rewarding, the behavior itself ceases.

One important remaining question is why you are the favorite. If it is because of your stellar performance, perhaps the favoritism indicates that you are a rising star in the organization. However, if there is no logical reason for the favoritism, be on guard because it can disappear in 15 minutes.

We owe you one

Q. For several months, my manager had been telling me that he was most likely going to give a very desirable work assignment to me. A few days ago, he gave it to one of his pets. All my manager said to me was, "We owe you one." What do you suggest I do now?
P.G.

On the credibility scale, "We owe you one," is right up there with, "The check is in the mail." The fact is that you are dealing with an unbelievable manager. As other choice assignments go to some of his other pets, don't be surprised to hear, "We owe you two or three or four."

If he were truly committed to keeping his commitments, he would have said more to you than some vague throwaway line. For example, if he had met with you, discussed the decision, and pointed out the kinds of specific opportunities that he will try to steer your way in the future, that would be a far better sign.

Because he did not discuss these opportunities with you, then you should discuss them with him. Meet with him and ask him to elaborate on just what it is that he owes you. Be sure to get his input regarding any actions that you should be taking in order to be fully qualified when such opportunities arise. As time passes, let him know about your successes.

Unfortunately, you are dealing with a manager who plays favorites, does not keep his word, and communicates marginally. You owe yourself something better than this.

Chapter
—9—

The Feedback Backlash

Although feedback is essential for learning and development, there are some individuals who use it as a weapon. They provide subordinates, peers, or even superiors with information that is inaccurate, unfounded, opinionated, overly evaluative, and often quite hurtful. By calling it feedback, they somehow think this provides them with license to say whatever they wish.

The irony is that the people who dole out this type of drivel could actually use some feedback themselves. They need to understand that their behavior qualifies them as jerks.

Fortunately, there are a number of steps that the recipients can take in order to move the process in a more positive and constructive direction.

No need to insult

Q. I came up with a good idea and mentioned it to my manager. She suggested I put it in writing. After a couple of weeks, she wrote a letter back to me saying the idea was useless and left her cold. I am annoyed and wonder if I should say something.
C.L.

It actually sounds like your manager's response was useless and left you cold. Regardless of any action you take, it is important to recognize at the outset that a person who writes this type of letter is not typically inclined to listen to constructive feedback.

Even if your idea was ridiculous, there is no excuse for her response. Her response has generated anger and squelched the likelihood of your ever presenting another creative idea to her. As a result, she loses, the company loses, and, unfortunately, you lose.

Because you are so upset over her reaction, you should meet with her. This should not be a meeting where you evaluate her or the letter, but rather one in which you try to clarify the ground rules. Tell her that you were confused by her response to your idea, and you would like to know if there is anything you should be doing in order to avoid this type of reaction in the future. Her reply will tell you if it is a good idea to continue in her department, or if it is a better idea to broaden your horizons.

A critical mass of criticism

Q. I don't know how to deal with a manager who is always criticizing my work. Every single day she is telling me that I did this or that wrong, and now whenever I see her, I brace myself for more criticism. What should I do?
W.H.

On a short-term basis, all you can do is brace yourself for more of the same. The irony in this situation is that your manager could be criticized every single day for her criticism of you. As a managerial approach, criticism tends to generate resistance, defensiveness, and dissatisfaction, and does nothing to correct the mistakes at hand. When employees are struggling, effective managers coach, counsel, and teach.

One step that may change her behavior starts with a careful look at your performance. Although it is normal for an employee to make mistakes along the way, if you are actually making key errors every day, you should ask yourself if you are doing everything in your power to be a highly effective employee. After all, the best way to reduce your manager's criticism is for you to make fewer errors.

In addition, the next time she criticizes your work, ask her for some specific guidance in order to prevent the problem in the future, and then be sure to incorporate her suggestions and let her know about any positive results. By letting her see that coaching is far more productive than criticizing, you may be able to have a positive impact on her performance as well as yours.

Name-calling

Q. We were having a staff meeting and I asked a basic question. After the meeting, my manager told me that he didn't want to embarrass me in front of the others, but my question was stupid. He feels he's a hero because he reprimanded me in private, but I'm annoyed over the criticism itself. What do you think?
E.S.

In Management 101, your manager gets half credit. He gets an "A" for providing negative feedback in private, and an "F" for the feedback itself.

The best managers today adhere to the adage that there is no such thing as a stupid question. It is not as if managers should be seeking so-called stupid questions, but it is through the opportunity to ask any question that innovation and creativity are fostered.

Your manager's actions can totally extinguish the employees' desire to think, take some mental risks, and approach problems in new and different ways. Even if you ask the most ridiculous question in the world, it is entirely possible that your question will generate some related ideas that can truly lead to more effective problem-solving. After all, some of the greatest ideas, concepts, and inventions started as stupid questions.

In addition, even if your question made absolutely no sense, the way that you were treated is ultimately going to prevent your associates from asking their own risky questions, and who is to say what creative ideas may be lost forever as a result? It's time for your manager to go back to Management 101.

Sticks and stones

Q. I just came out of a meeting with my manager where he described me as the "ringleader" in my department. The people I work with certainly listen to me, but I am upset with the ringleader label. How can I change it?
B.W.

Although being described as a ringleader is not a ringing endorsement of your effectiveness as an employee, it is not a death knell either. In fact, the good news is that your manager views you as a leader. This means that he believes you have some power relative to your fellow employees, and you are able to exert a degree of influence over them.

The problem is that your manager believes that, as an informal leader, you are using your skills to somehow induce your fellow employees to work against him. You should try to look very carefully at any actions that your fellow employees may have taken as a result of your suggestions, guidance, or direction. To the extent that you have played an intentional or unintentional role in steering the group away from what the manager wants, you have most likely merited that ringleader label.

The fact that your manager discussed this matter with you can be interpreted as a good sign, and it can be an indicator of his confidence in you. After all, many companies have done very well by promoting informal leaders. The real message is for you to be sure that your manager sees that the leadership you exert clearly supports departmental objectives. This approach can help take the ring out of ringleader.

The data dump

Q. The other day, my manager walked into my work area and said she wanted to give me some feedback. She then took out a piece of paper and read off a list of things that I have done wrong over the past three months. This was not my formal evaluation, and I am very upset by this treatment. What should I do?
R.L.

Feedback is essential for motivation, learning, and performance improvement, and it seems that feedback is quite necessary in your situation. It is your manager, however, that needs it. The notion of taking out a laundry list of stale complaints and dumping them on an unsuspecting employee is not even mismanagement. It is non-management.

If this is how your manager provides feedback, there may well be many other gaps in her managerial skills. As a result, there will probably be several instances in which you can actually help educate her and help the department at large.

You should discuss the matter with your manager, but do not criticize her. Let her know that you are definitely interested in improving the quality and quantity of your work, and you appreciate any feedback that can help you meet this objective. In this regard, be sure to add that you would like to receive such feedback as close as possible to the behavior in question.

It is particularly important to meet with your manager as soon as possible. If you delay, then you are not providing prompt feedback for her questionable behavior.

Who has a bad attitude?

Q. Over the last few months, my supervisor has told me several times that I have a bad attitude. I disagree with this, and when I try to explain, she does not listen. The incidents that she uses as examples are totally out of context. How should I deal with this?
A.T.

When employees are told that they have negative attitudes, their typical reaction is to become even more negative. This, of course, leads to further comments about their attitude, which in turns leads to further negativity. Fortunately, there are ways to stop this cycle before it carries you away.

One step is to honestly determine whether you have a negative attitude. Try to think of any behaviors that could be interpreted as being at odds with your supervisor. This does not have to be a major battle, but can be testy comments, cutting questions, or defensive body language.

In addition, it is time to discuss the issue with your supervisor in more detail. Tell her that if she sees situations that point to negative attitudes on your part, you would like to know about them and correct them at that time. Be sure that you adequately publicize your behaviors that demonstrate a positive attitude. After all, the best indicator of attitude is behavior, and it will be very important to let her see that you are not misbehaving.

Unflattering descriptors

Q. Practically every time I come into the office, my manager tells me that I look upset. I am not, and I don't hear this from anyone else at work. Is there any significance to it?
A.W.

One very good way to get people upset is to tell them they look upset. No matter how an employee feels, this type of comment causes many people to instantly wonder about their smile, eyes, hair, clothes, and body language, so it's off to the bathroom for a quick check with the mirror.

Presumably your fellow employees are at least as open with you as your manager, so it is revealing that they are not giving you this type of feedback. This raises one question: Is there something about being in the presence of your manager that is upsetting you? You may want to think a little more about your working relationship with him, along with the possibility that you may be telegraphing some dissatisfaction in this area.

If you are unable to find anything that could be triggering this reaction from your manager, it is possible that your manager is personally upset with something, and, as a result, he is more likely to think that others are upset. There is also a possibility that he is upset with something about your work, and this is his way of expressing it.

It may be helpful for you to meet with him and tell him that you are not upset with anything at work, but you are concerned that he thinks you are. The matter may end there, or he may give you a valuable piece of feedback about yourself or a piece of insight into him. Either way, this is nothing that should upset you.

A manner of speaking

Q. My manager shocked me yesterday when she said I should do something about my manners. I am a polite person and my manners are fine. When I asked her to be more specific, she did not give me one concrete example. I haven't a clue as to what to do now.
J.T.

In a manner of speaking, it sounds like your manager is the one who is clueless over the issue of manners. Simply telling a person that he or she has bad manners is not going to win any Golden Napkins or whatever awards may exist for politeness. In addition, by putting up a stone wall when asked to elaborate on her comments, your manager is not exactly in line for any managerial awards, either.

Your best step is to revisit her on this matter. If there are some problems with your manners, you need to know precisely what they are so that you can correct them. And if there are no real problems in this area, you need to find out what is behind her comments.

If you have reviewed your manners and honestly believe that nothing is missing, that is precisely what you should tell your manager. Let her know that you take her comments seriously, and you would like her help in putting together a game plan to improve any aspects of your work behavior that may not be up to par.

Her response should put the whole matter of manners into focus. On the one hand, you may get some valuable feedback. On the other hand, as you listen to her, remember that the weaknesses that people see in others are often indicative of their own short-comings. This situation may be telling you more about your manager than about your manners.

An unflattering image

Q. I manage a group of 10 employees, and I thought we had a solid team. However, this morning someone placed a cartoon on my desk depicting a complete buffoon running a meeting. I'm miffed by the cartoon and equally concerned that someone felt they had to give it to me anonymously. What do you suggest I do?
N.B.

The one move to avoid is anything that smacks of managerial buffoonery. This means that you will be doing yourself a real dis-service if you tear into the cartoon at a meeting or play sleuth and try to figure out who sent it.

You should look at the act in its context. It sounds like things are working relatively well in your group, and this is an isolated incident. You are probably correct in assuming that whoever dropped it off is less than delighted, but it is not as if there is an insurrection. If you are a manager who communicates with the employees, listens to their ideas and suggestions, and respects their needs, you should not give the incident or the cartoon another thought, unless it signals the start of a trend.

At this point, one employee sent one message. Do not overreact and give more employees a reason to think your management style should be accompanied by a horn and seltzer bottle.

How much professional distance?

Q. My boss just told me that I am "too nice" to the customers, and I should maintain more professional distance. I'm a friendly person, and I don't see a problem with the way I act. I'm not sure what to do now.
B.A.

The expression, "too nice," can mean too many things. On the one hand, the argument can be made that you can never be too nice to the customers, particularly in today's age of service. On the other hand, being "too nice" can mean that you have gone too far.

If you truly see no problem with the way you relate to the customers, the next step is to go back to your boss and tell him the same. Ask him for some specific examples of situations in which your behavior was inappropriate, and then ask him for some guidance as to the way that he would like you to act in such situations.

It is possible that your behavior has gone over the top, and this may be very helpful guidance. At the same time, perhaps your behavior is appropriate, but not for your kind of work or customers. Or, perhaps the problem is not with your behavior at all, but rather with your boss.

Pay careful attention to your boss's comments, as they can provide you with information that can help you do some career planning, and that's nice, too.

Cryptic comments

Q. The other day my manager looked at me in front of a group of employees and said, "Nice suit. I wish I could afford one like that." I'm not paranoid, but I keep thinking about what he's really trying to say. I wonder if he is telling me that I'm being paid too much or if he thinks I'm too showy. How do you interpret this?
A.S.

It sounds like you have a nice suit. If you really want to know what your manager is telling you, put his comments into the work context. Take a look at other comments that he has made to you and see if this fits into a pattern. For example, if he has been giving you negative feedback regarding the way that you are perceived by your fellow employees, then this may be more of the same message. It is also helpful to consider whether this type of inane comment is typical of him or if he has been singling you out for particular innuendoes.

In a word, his comment can be interpreted as an insult or as a compliment. If there is nothing else in your work relationship that tells you he is concerned about your style, then you should regard the remark as nothing more than a throwaway line.

Parlor games

Q. As part of the entertainment at our year-end dinner, the company hired a handwriting analyst. She came to the table where I was sitting with my manager and several fellow employees and asked us to write our names on a sheet of paper. Then she gave some positive descriptions of everyone except me. She wondered about my energy and persistence. I don't know if my manager bought what she was saying, but he semi-jokingly said that he would like to hire her to help screen new applicants. This experience wrecked the whole evening for me, and I'm wondering if I should discuss the matter with him.
L.E.

Just because a handwriting analyst had a less-than-flattering description of you does not mean that the handwriting is on the wall. This person was part of the evening's entertainment, and you should leave it at that. Your persistence and energy levels are best reflected by your performance on the job, rather than by someone who does not have one fact concerning your work.

Every once in a while, one hears about a company that uses handwriting analysis in the hiring process. The positive side of handwriting analysis is that it typically provides attractively bound reports with definitive statements regarding numerous aspects of a person's personality, such as confidence, maturity, intelligence, independence, and so forth. The only problem is that there is no scientific basis behind these assertions.

There have been studies in which the exact same handwriting samples have been sent to different handwriting analysts and the reports from these analysts reached totally different conclusions about the personality of the writer. Handwriting analysis is interesting, intriguing, and amusing, and its role in business is just where you found it—as entertainment at a year-end dinner.

There is no reason for you to meet with your manager to discuss the comments made by this entertainer. For whatever reason, she picked up some inaccurate cues from you. Perhaps it was your attire, pattern of speech, or the way you were sitting. Although she was analyzing your handwriting, she was looking at you and trying to gather as much data as possible.

When it comes to work, handwriting content is far more important than style, parlor games belong in the parlor, and the most accurate indicator of a person's energy level is his or her behavior. Speaking of behavior, do you think a low-energy person would write a letter?

A little too personal

Q. I am a dental hygienist and I have been working for a group of dentists for more than five years. Last week we were told that a consulting firm was going to evaluate our practice. We filled out a questionnaire that asked how we felt about everyone in the office, but then we were supposed to fill out a personality test that has very personal questions. I am afraid of being fired for not filling it out. What recourse do I have if they fire me for being "uncooperative?"
T.F.

There is an irony in having your personality labeled "uncooperative" because you refused to take a test that is designed to learn about your personality. If you are fired for this refusal, your legal recourse will depend on the totality of circumstances associated with the termination, and you would need to review the entire matter with an attorney.

At the same time, regardless of what management may or may not do to you, there are some important issues that need your attention. In the first place, you have been working for this group for more than five years, yet you are concerned about immediate termination for one arguably defensible action. The fact that you feel you could be terminated under these circumstances sends some very questionable messages about the skills, effectiveness, and values of your employer.

In addition, although it makes perfectly good sense for your employer to retain outside experts to help improve operations, it is important that these types of projects include numerous opportunities for two-way communication. You cannot be the only employee who is upset by having to complete a test that includes private issues that are unrelated to the job. The real question is why you cannot sit down with management and discuss your concerns.

The final issue deals with the test itself. Many paper-and-pencil personality tests are clinical tools that can be quite effective when people seek personal and confidential help from a trained professional. However, when used in the work setting, many of these instruments are easy to fake, unrelated to the job, upsetting to the employees, and often lacking in validity and reliability.

It appears that one key issue in your organization is a lack of communication between the employees and management, and this is where you, as well as the consultants, should be placing more emphasis.

No one's perfect

Q. I have been doing excellent work, but my manager just gave me all fours on a five-point scale. When I asked why, he said, "No one's perfect." I don't think that's fair. What should I do?
D.F.

When it comes to understanding the role of feedback, your manager gets a minus 10 on your five-point scale. Although technically no one is perfect, there can certainly be perfect behavior. After all, if you get 10 out of 10 correct on a test, it's a perfect score.

The first step is to ask your manager if there are any actions that you can take to earn a five. Try to establish some measurable goals with him, along with the expectation that you will receive a five if you meet them.

In addition, many evaluation forms provide the employee with the opportunity to write some comments. This is not the time for a flaming tirade against your manager, but rather a chance to describe your specific achievements and the extent to which you met or even exceeded departmental standards and objectives. This should be written in positive and constructive terms.

If you are concerned that your evaluation may work against you when an opportunity for promotion arises, remember that your manager is probably well-known as a tough grader. The fact that you earned all fours may be regarded as a perfectly acceptable accomplishment.

Chapter
—10—

With Friends Like This

People often think that it would be nothing short of terrific to work with their friends. After all, they get along, communicate well, understand each other, and share some common interests. In many ways, working with friends would seem to be an effective way to build a solid work force. The argument is that friendship sets the foundation for strong teams. However, it can also set the foundation for strong arguments, cliques, and conflicts.

Working side-by-side with friends brings an emotional element into the workplace that can ignite any number of issues. Problems that are strictly work-related suddenly take on an emotional charge. For example, when an acquaintance at work makes a mistake that affects a co-worker, there can be a businesslike discussion and review to correct the problem. When a friend does this to a friend, the major underlying question often focuses less on work issues and more on whether the friendship can survive intact. Working with friends can interfere with communication, discipline, teamwork, productivity, and much more.

One piece of friendly advice is that when working with friends, the focus should be on the body of work, rather than on the buddies at work.

They're happy for you...sort of

Q. I was just promoted over several of my friends, and now they hardly talk to me. I thought they would be happy for me, but I was sure wrong about that. I wonder why I even tried for this promotion. What should I do?
R.A.

Unfortunately, there are many people who sense that a step forward for their friends is a step backward for themselves. The good news is these feelings subside in time.

You are in the middle of what can be called promotion commotion. There are all sorts of initial stresses, strains, and pains for those who are promoted, as well as for those who are not. Resistance from former co-workers is a common part of the process.

People in your position often fall into the trap of missing the good old days, and some consider giving up the promotion and returning to the pack. They rationalize that they do not have what it takes to be in supervision.

Someone in your company believes that you have the wherewithal to make it as a leader, and it is important to recognize that you may not be able to make an accurate assessment for yourself until several months have passed. Don't be tempted to make this assessment in the first few days...or hours...or minutes.

Looking at your situation a little differently, would you rather be promoted over co-workers who are your friends or your enemies? Although there are some advantages in being promoted over friends, it is important to accept the fact that your friendships with your former co-workers has permanently changed. You can still be a friendly leader, but if you try to be a buddy as well as a supervisor, you will fail at both.

This is also a good time to honestly answer one question: Has the promotion gone to your head? If it has, you may as well be promoted over your enemies, because that is just what they will become.

The best thing to do now is keep the lines of communication open with the troops and let them see the qualities they valued in you as a friend—your openness, fairness, responsiveness, and concern for them. Many of the traits that made you a good friend are the same ones that can help make you a good leader.

The unfriendly friend

Q. A fellow employee whom I considered a friend was in a position to help me get an assignment he knows I wanted. I heard from a reliable source that he did not stand up for me, but pushed for someone else, and then he lied to me about what he had said. I'm very upset and wonder if I should say something.
S.M.

Before you take any action, you need to be absolutely certain as to who is dealing with facts and who is dealing with fiction. It is possible that your friend was telling you the truth, and the reliable source is not so reliable.

If there is no doubt that your friend acted in an unfriendly way, you should take a look at how much the situation is eating away at you. Although it may be tempting to say something, try to envision what that conversation would be like.

You can expect nervousness, tension, defensiveness, and even a heated argument. Your friendship is already severed, and this follow-up encounter could sever the working relationship, too. And, you could end up being labeled as disgruntled or out of control. Although you may let off some steam, you may be the one who gets burned.

You are better off focusing on your performance and whether your successes are being adequately publicized. By doing this, the next time a choice assignment comes along, you will be a more obvious choice, and you will not have to rely on the whims of those who have no idea of what it means to be a friend.

A friendly referral

Q. I referred one of my friends to work here. The company brought him on board, but he made some foolish mistakes and was terminated in a matter of weeks. Our friendship survived, but can this type of incident hurt my credibility in the company?
A.B.

Just about any problematic incident linked to your name can hurt your credibility, but that certainly does not mean that it will. Step one is to take a look at the actual mistakes that led to your friend's tailspin. If he was just mismatched in the job, this can happen under any hiring circumstances and there is no reason for people to raise questions about you. On the other hand, if other people around the office use language more colorful than "foolish" to describe his mistakes, such as words like despicable, heinous, or outrageous, then there may indeed be a few questions about your judgment, at least when it comes to selecting friends.

Perhaps one other key reason for fingers to be pointed in your direction would be your track record as a referral source. If you have been referring numerous friends to the company, and their average tenure is best measured in hours, then your credibility may encounter some turbulence.

Short of the kinds of scenarios noted, there is no way for anyone to reasonably think any less of you because of your friend's failure. To the contrary, many employers know that one of the most effective sources of better applicants is through their better employees. These applicants come prescreened, and many of the possible unknowns are already well-known.

Employers also recognize that the entire hiring process is based on probabilities. There are numerous factors that can raise the probability of making a successful employment decision, and hiring a friend of a solid employee often raises the odds a few points. However, even with the most thorough and comprehensive screening techniques, hiring mistakes are made. Rather than trying to attribute blame when this occurs, many companies try to analyze why it occurred, and then develop some specific strategies to prevent this kind of mismatch in the future.

Having carefully watched your friend's entry and exit from the company, you may have some valuable advice for management in this area.

Just sign here

Q. Several of my friends at work asked me to sign a petition complaining about our manager. The petition will be directed to the president of the company. Granted our manager is a problem, but I am hesitant to sign the petition because of difficulties this may cause for me later. However, I don't want my friends to be upset with me. What do you suggest I do?
P.H.

It is important to be true to your friends, but you need to be true to yourself first. If you have concerns or fears regarding possible negative ramifications associated with signing the petition, you should tell your friends exactly how you feel. And, you should not sign it.

If you sign the petition, the most likely scenario is that you are going to be thinking about it constantly, and there will be nothing any friend can say that will put your mind at ease.

It is true that your friends may become upset with you because you did not sign, even if you take a pop-psychology approach and tell them that you are against the petition and not against them. However, friendships are living entities, and they go through periods of sickness and health, closeness and distance, and ups and downs. Your decision may alter your present relationship with these co-workers, but if the friendship is based on more than work expediency, there will soon be other decisions that can start the healing process.

At the same time, if your decision causes these co-workers to refuse to be friendly to you, then the friendship was not built on much of a foundation. True friends respect each other's needs, wishes, and differences. If this is not the case with your fellow employees, then they were neither true nor friends.

On a broader basis, when employees start signing and sending petitions to top management, it is actually an indication of larger communication problems. Your manager is one such problem, and your company's leadership appears to lack the accessibility to be aware of it. The actions that topside leadership takes in response to the petition will tell you a great deal about the company, just as the actions of your friends will tell you a great deal about the company you keep.

The broken confidence

Q. I was upset with one of my fellow employees, and I made a comment about her in confidence to one of my friends at work. My friend broke our trust and told her what I said. I'm very upset and don't know what to do now.
N.D.

These days, you can take back all kinds of things, such as clothing, electronic equipment, or even a car...but you still cannot take back the spoken word. For better or worse, you are having a "learning experience." Although such an experience is often a codeword for a failure, all that it means is that you failed in a particular situation, but you are not a total failure unless you repeat the behavior that brought you here in the first place.

In the meantime, there are some actions that you can take. On the preventive side, if you are ever in doubt as to whether you should say or do anything, picture how it would look on the front page of this newspaper the next day. Whether dealing with a business issue or not, Murphy's Law still applies: If something can go wrong, it will. And, don't forget Murphy's Corollary: Not only will things go wrong, they will do so at the worst possible time.

As for what to do now, instead of looking at this as a bad dream, it makes far more sense to refocus things and recognize that this is a real opportunity to grow. First, take a look at yourself and try to honestly see what caused you to make the less-than-flattering remark about your fellow employee in the first place. By looking at what you see as a weakness in others, you stand a real chance of identifying a weakness in yourself.

Secondly, until you clear the air with this individual, you will continue to feel uncomfortable. The best way to find relief is to seriously consider approaching her and apologizing. After all, if you are satisfied that you made a mistake, the best thing to do is to correct it.

You and this person will not necessarily bond into lifelong friends as a result, but at least the heavy air of tension for both of you will be dissipated and you can put your attention where it belongs: on your work.

And, at some point along the way, you may want to talk things over with your former friend.

The borrower

Q. There is one person I work with whom I regard as a friend, but he is always borrowing from me, and he rarely returns them. I have a lot of regular contact with him, and I don't want to create a problem by saying "no." What should I do?
L.C.

Most people remember the Shakespearean line, "Neither a borrower, nor a lender be." However, it is equally important to remember the very next line in this quote: "For loan oft loses both itself and friend...." The bottom line is that if you want to keep your friend and your things, it is time to close the lending office.

If this person is really a friend, you can be honest with him. Let him know that it is upsetting to lend things to him and never see them again. Tell him that you think he should build up his inventory of items needed for the job, and add that you are willing to help him select whatever he needs.

Part of being a friend is to help your friends develop into stronger individuals. Although it may initially seem that you are going to create a bigger problem by refusing to lend things to him, the fact is that you are going to create bigger problems if you continue to do so. You are going to become increasingly upset, and it will just be a matter of time before your anger explodes.

Do not wait to take this action until your friend asks to borrow something. Rather, approach him now and tell him that you want to prevent a future problem. If he is a real friend, he will appreciate your efforts to help him and the friendship.

The friendship-promoting program

Q. Our company has a "secret pal" program where each employee is anonymously paired with another employee, and they are supposed to send each other little gifts. Most of the people I work with cannot stand this program. Is this a typical reaction, and what should we do from here?
W.M.

The best-kept secret about "secret pal" programs is that they may actually interfere with employee attitudes, cooperation, and morale. A program that is very cute for building friendships between kindergartners does not typically merit the same happy face in the world of business.

In fact, these programs are often viewed as a source of aggravation. One employee spends time tracking down a perfect little book for his or her secret pal, only to get a dog-eared candy bar left over from last Halloween in return.

If you and your co-workers have been keeping your attitudes toward the secret pal program a secret, the time has come to let the truth out. Tell management how you feel and suggest an alternative approach. For example, you can suggest that management form a task force of employees to review and present some motivational programs that they would like to see implemented. Because of these employees' input, there is a far greater likelihood that such programs will be appropriate and effective.

If companies want to build teamwork and turn employees into pals, there should be no secrets.

I get a bad feeling about this

Q. One of my friends at work recently signed up with a multi-level marketing organization and wants me to do likewise. The products seem fine, but my "gut feel" is that this is not for me. She keeps telling me to forget about "gut feel" and listen to the facts. The only reason I would join is that I don't want to lose a friend. What should I do?
R.S.

It is impossible for you to lose a friend if you do not rush with open arms and phone lines to join her budding empire. The reason is that if this person is no longer friendly with you after you decline her offer, she was not really your friend in the first place, and you can't lose what you didn't have.

Your friend keeps advising you to listen to the facts, but if she really believes that, she is missing an important one herself: Research has found that some of the most powerful and effective decision-makers actually rely heavily on "gut feel."

"Gut feel" is the result of your mind putting the present decision through a filter made up of all of your experiences over the years. The result is that you get a visceral reaction to the decision: Either you can stomach it or you cannot.

This means that your experience is telling you to pass on this, even if your friend's multi-level company has the perfect antacid to quell your nervous stomach.

At the same time, it sounds like you have been expressing some uncertainty to your friend as to whether you will or will not join. As long as she senses that the door is even slightly open, she will keep trying to squeeze through.

The time has come to tell her that you have made a decision— no wavering, no equivocating, and no procrastinating. You can thank her for letting you look over the opportunity, and you can honestly tell her that you hope it is successful for her...but it is not an opportunity that you wish to pursue, and you hope that she will understand. You can also tell her you hope that your friendship will continue intact.

It is said that you cannot put a price on friendship, and you are about to see if that is true.

Some sort of friend

Q. I came up with a good idea to improve the way that our department works, and I mentioned it to one of my friends here. The next thing I knew, she presented it to our manager. He thinks the idea is terrific, and now my friend is some sort of hero. What should I do?
N.S.

The first thing to do is open the dictionary and look up the word "friend." You are actually talking about an acquaintance, and even that is a stretch. Before your manager commissions a sculptor to make a statue of her, you need to sit down with her and have a little chat.

The best approach is to use a low-key, assertive, and business-like style. Your opening comments should focus on her specific behavior that you found to be so questionable—namely, her taking your idea to management. The idea was yours and she had no right to do this. The next step is to tell her how you feel about her actions. Let her know that this was upsetting and stressful, and you feel hurt and betrayed.

Having set this groundwork, you should then suggest that the two of you meet with the manager to discuss the matter. Let her know that both of you will look better in the manager's eyes if you sit down with him and honestly explain what happened.

If she categorically refuses to do this, tell her that you plan to approach the manager on your own. Incidentally, if you happen to have any kind of proof that the idea was yours, let her know that you will be bringing it with you. In your meeting with the manager, one effective approach is to tell him that you have a problem at work and you would like his help in solving it. Then describe the entire incident. If he is any kind of a manager, he will start his investigation immediately.

The larger question for you is whether you are afraid to act assertively. Being assertive is not being aggressive or obnoxious; it is merely standing up for your rights and beliefs. If you don't do so, it is quite likely that there will be others who steal ideas and opportunities that are rightfully yours.

Unfriendly persuasion

Q. One of the people I'm friendly with at work is not happy with this company, and she wants me to join her when she complains to management. I don't think things are that bad, and I've told her this, but she keeps trying to convince me. How do I get her to stop?
S.P.

It is interesting that you describe your fellow employee as one of the people you are "friendly with." You are probably a person who likes to be friendly with everyone and have everyone like you. Part of that package includes a tendency to spend extra hours listening to others and sympathizing with them. The downside is that these traits make you a magnet for chronic complainers.

By being regularly accessible and willing to discuss the goings-on in the company, you are inadvertently indicating that you could be persuaded to her way of thinking. Your patience and understanding are being misinterpreted by the complainer as agreement. This means that you are actually rewarding her constant attempts to persuade you, and, as a result, she is repeating these behaviors.

If you want her to stop trying to convince you to join her on her perilous trip to management, you need to stop discussing the merits and demerits of the company with her. The next time she approaches you and starts the tirade, use a more direct approach: Tell her that you understand her dissatisfaction, but you do not share the same feelings, and you have absolutely no interest in accompanying her to discuss any of this with management.

Although it might be nice to think that you should tell her that you would be more than willing to discuss ways to help her resolve her complaints on her own, such a discussion will more than likely gravitate right back to her belief that the problems cannot be solved without complaining to management and, once again, you should be joining her in this escapade. At some point, she needs to know that no means no.

Two against one

Q. For the past year, I have been working in a small office with one other person. We worked well together until two months ago when a new employee was brought on to join us. She befriended my co-worker, and now it's the two of them against me. I am upset with both of them, and I'm not sure what to do now.
D.S.

You are perched in the middle of two separate situations that social scientists have often found to be rather antisocial. In the first place, groups composed of three people are often noted to be particularly troublesome. While two people can work comfortably and productively together, it is not uncommon to find that groups of three soon fall into a two-against-one scenario.

Secondly, social scientists often point to increased levels of stress, tension, and aggressiveness in crowded settings. Because your office was fairly small prior to the arrival of your new co-worker, the tightened working conditions are probably adding to your level of distress.

The first step is to formulate a clear picture of the amount of time you are actually being ignored, overlooked, or excluded by your fellow employees. After all, there are times when people in any group occasionally feel that they are being left out.

If you find that you are being left out more than left in, the next step is to meet with your co-workers to discuss the problem. The idea is to review the specific instances that upset you and then suggest some ways for the three of you to work more amicably and effectively together.

This type of situation will improve in direct proportion to the amount of communication among the players. Because you are the odd person out, it will be up to you to initiate much of the dialogue in this area. At the same time, remember that the future can bring a realignment of alliances among the three of you, along with the possibility of having more employees in your cozy little department.

It is also worth remembering that management does not like situations that upset or divide the employees. If you find that your one-on-two meetings with your co-workers are having no impact, perhaps it is time for a one-on-one meeting with your manager.

Chapter
—11—

Pros
and Conflicts

Conflicts are inevitable as soon as two people start working with each other, because it does not take much for them to start working against each other. Conflicts are found at all levels of an organization, and they can run the gamut from an unfriendly glance to a full-scale battle.

It can be argued that conflict is healthy for an organization. It is sometimes true that conflict indicates that an organization is vital, dynamic, and changing. When people disagree, they're thinking and this is fertile ground for a broad range of improvements.

In a basic sense, there is a good deal of truth associated with the positive aspects of conflict. However, when the conflict moves away from animated discussion and disagreement, and toward hostility and aggression, it is not healthy for any individual or organization.

Because conflicts with departments, managers, subordinates, associates, cliques, and even with customers are inevitable, it is important for people at any job level to recognize that they have the power to manage many aspects of this discord. The key step in the process is to understand how to make conflicts constructive rather than destructive.

The feeling isn't mutual

Q. I have two important employees that work for me, and it is essential for them to work together. However, they do not like each other at all, and I am concerned about what this will do to their productivity. Is there a way to help them get along better?
S.F.

As a manager, the best place to focus attention is on your employees' work, rather than on their work relationships. Just because employees dislike each other is not an automatic cause for alarm. It may signal a future decline in productivity, or it may not.

There are some employees who are as close as the Hatfields and the McCoys, but they put aside their dislike and focus their attention on doing their work. They recognize that there is a job to be done, and if they do not like particular co-workers, that is a fact but not a problem. At the same time, there are other employees who put their work aside and focus their attention on disliking each other. These employees devote a major effort toward disliking a particular co-worker, and this type of behavior is not only disruptive, it can be contagious.

Before taking any action, you need to determine the impact that your employees' mutual dislike is having on their performance. There are cases of organizations that have been very successful in spite of less-than-amicable relations among employees. This is not to make an argument for having a work environment that resembles a war zone, but it further indicates that the key focus should be on productivity and not personality.

However, if their dislike starts to interfere with their work or that of their fellow employees, then it is time for concern. The first step is to bring the two of them together and review the specific problems emanating from their behavior. Indicate that the situation is unacceptable, and then ask them what they are going to do individually and together in order to correct it.

The next step is to indicate that you want them to jointly develop a specific plan to correct these work problems. By completing this plan, they are far more likely to be committed to it, and it may help increase their commitment to each other.

Arguing again

Q. Two of my co-workers do not get along, and whenever our manager is out, which happens often, they start arguing. I don't want to be branded as a person who runs to the manager whenever there is a problem, but this situation is upsetting everyone in the office. What should I do?
R.T.

When your co-workers would rather punch each other than punch a time clock, this is an issue that needs to be discussed with your manager. There is a real problem in your department, and any responsible manager would like to know about it.

It sounds like you are overly concerned about being branded as a corporate crier if you go to management. If it makes you more comfortable, you can certainly try to intervene and resolve the problem yourself, but remember that the battle can easily move from two combatants to three.

The better option is for you to join forces with several of your fellow employees and then meet with your manager. After all, your co-workers sound like they are as upset with the war zone as you are.

At the core of the problem is your manager's frequent absence from the office. Because the main responsibilities of a manager are to manage, this is not easily accomplished from afar.

In your meeting with the manager, you can approach the problem of the battling employees in the same way that you would discuss any other matter that is interfering with your ability to do your job. However, your less-obvious message is that your department needs more regular supervision, either by the manager or by someone acting in his or her behalf.

At present, it sounds like no one has been designated as assistant manager or acting manager, or somebody has dropped the ball. It will be important for your manager to be sure that someone is formally empowered in an acting leadership role, with full authority to oversee the department during the manager's absence.

The warring employees in your department already know how to get along—they do it whenever the manager is present. If they can act this well in front of a manager, their performance should be even more compelling in front of an acting manager.

The unkind cuts

Q. There is one particular person that I work with on many projects. Whenever someone from management is around, she always has some little cutting remark about my performance. What's the best way to deal with her?
C.D.

In a word, the best way to deal with her is from a distance. After all, she does not work with you; she works against you.

If the two of you absolutely must work together, there are a few steps to take before the project begins. First, you should tell her that you are not going to sit quietly while she trashes you in front of management. When she looks at you in shock and wonders how you could ever think such a thought, you should give her specific examples of the kinds of put-downs that you will no longer tolerate.

Secondly, if she still blasts you in front of management, you need to express your dissatisfaction on the spot. This does not mean selecting the yelling-and-screaming option. If you really want to be heard at work, it is best to remember that you are in a business environment and need to act in a businesslike manner. You should calmly yet firmly indicate that you would like to clarify a few issues regarding her comments. At that point, you should present a few irrefutable facts that vividly demonstrate the inaccuracy of her criticisms.

At the same time, her put-downs raise an underlying issue for you: How well are you marketing yourself on the job? While your co-worker's idea of self-promotion is to try to toss you into the dumpster, you can be using a more positive approach to advance your cause.

As you meet or exceed work objectives or individual developmental goals, it is useful to ask yourself if management is aware of your accomplishments. Although many companies have elaborate tracking systems in this area, some have cracks that resemble the Grand Canyon. Part of your job will be to fill them.

A final point to keep in mind is that many managers know that employees who trash their co-workers typically have more problems than a math final.

Take, take, take

Q. I am in sales, and I have a good customer who keeps asking for unpromised favors, reports, or analyses that require extra work by me. Is there a way to cut this back and keep them as a customer? C.R.

This is an era where sales and service are critically intertwined in most industries, and if you try to cut back your service, your customer may decide to cut back your sales. In fact, it is entirely possible that one key reason why you have this good customer in the first place is the service you provide.

Many products call for considerable follow-up support by a salesperson and his or her company. Importantly, the first place to look in trying to solve your dilemma is at your company, rather than at your customer. The broader question is whether your company is providing you with adequate support when it comes to meeting the needs of all of your customers after the sales have been made.

Although you can certainly expect to spend at least some of your time helping and guiding your customers, there may be some steps your company can take to reduce the amount of time in which you need to be directly involved. It may be helpful to group your customers' requests into categories, and then meet with management to discuss ways in which their requests can be handled more effectively.

By taking this approach, you can actually improve the service that your customers receive, and you will be doing a service for your own company as well.

Politically incorrect

Q. My manager's political views are very different from mine, and I am concerned that if he finds out, my chances for promotion are going to suffer. Whenever a group of us talk politics, such as at lunch, I nod and say very little. I'm not happy about this, but I don't want to hurt my chances to advance. Is there a better way to handle this?
P.F.

Are you in a company whose leadership is waiting to pounce on any employees whose opinions differ from the established corporate line? No matter what else may be going on in the company, you should not plan on working in any firm where a self-imposed gag order is needed for survival.

This means that your first step is to determine the accuracy of your perception about the company's tolerance for political views that differ from those of the topsiders. The indirect way to do this is to take a careful look at the employees who have advanced in the firm, and compare them with those who have either left the firm or had minimal upward mobility in it.

When you look at the management team, are there all kinds of varied descriptors that best depict them, or can you describe the whole bunch of them in just a few words? If they are a narrow group, your chances of success are narrower.

You can also consider taking a more direct approach to validating your perception. You don't have to stand on top of your desk and call a noon rally for your cause, but the next time you are in a political discussion, you should lose the gag, stop the nodding, and express some of your thoughts.

It will not take long for you to start receiving some signs as to whether your opinions have singled you out as an independent, confident, and self-assured individual, or as simply a troublemaker who does not fit into the corporate mold. Many progressive companies today place a premium on diversity and the dynamic environment that it fosters. Once you determine whether your company encourages diversity or fights it, your decision will be an easy one.

Reacting to an overreaction

Q. One of my fellow managers charged into my office and started ranting and raving about how one of my employees made some mistakes and caused his employees to be late on our joint project. I barked back at him, and I knew immediately that was a mistake. What is the best way to handle this type of situation?
J.H.

When managers come charging into fellow managers' offices in a rant-and-rave mode, this does not exactly qualify them for rave reviews from the American Management Association. At the same time, you are correct in thinking that it was not a great idea to get into barking contest with him.

Looking first at the actual situation, the best approach for you to take when encountering this type of verbal attack is to listen, let him recite his litany, and then take the one step that can help resolve the matter: Tell him that you will look into the situation immediately and get back to him as soon as possible. After all, when he is going through his tirade, you have no way of knowing if his facts concerning your employee are accurate. There is not much of a basis for a discussion or an argument until you have checked out the situation.

After you have conducted your investigation, the next step is to meet with this manager and present him with facts, documentation, and a suggested plan of correction, whether or not the problem was caused by your employee. After all, it is a joint project.

The real issue is that your two departments depend upon each other on various projects, but it sounds like there has been minimal managerial communication and coordination during such projects. The best way to avoid this kind of problem in the future is for the two of you to establish a more formalized timetable that calls for status meetings at several points along the way.

When there are surprises at the end of an interdepartmental project, they are typically symptoms of a lack of adequate managerial communication and follow-up. And, speaking of communication, you and your fellow manager should discuss the blow-up that occurred and commit yourselves to talk rather than rant, rave, or bark if problems develop.

A little too cute

Q. One of my co-workers can get obnoxious and make comments that he thinks are cute, but they're not. I read that in this type of situation, a person should act the same way right back and that will get the offensive comments to stop. Do you agree?
L.A.

Comments that are obnoxious and supposedly cute actually sound like harassment, and the last thing that is going to stop a harasser is more harassment. If you want him to stop, you need to be direct.

By making some equally obnoxious comments in return, all you will be doing is placing yourself in an escalating verbal joust. Rather than stopping him, your volley will just encourage him to try even harder to top you. In essence, you will be increasing the unpleasant behavior, rather than decreasing it.

And, if you decide at some point to report the matter to your manager, how will you feel when this person relates some of the obnoxious comments that you made to him? He could even play victim.

If someone is making these kinds of comments to you, the best approach is to let the individual know your feelings about the comments, be specific about the behavior that must be stopped, and then add that you hope you will not have to take any further action on this matter.

The idea of using the same behavior as an obnoxious co-worker has a catchy visual appeal, but it does not work. And, if you do so, you might not work either.

The dueling duo

Q. Most of the departments under me work well together, but there are two that do not get along. I have worked with the department managers on this problem, but to no avail. We have brought these employees together specifically to improve their working relationship, but all they do is bicker. How do we get them to work as a team?
R.A.

When employees seem to focus more on screams than teams, the first step is to look at the departmental leadership, just as you have done. Be sure to look for any fundamental disagreements between these leaders, as they can easily spill over and undermine cooperation.

It is also important to see if there are structural factors causing problems between these departments. For example, does the company have any competitive programs or contests that may inadvertently place these departments in conflict with each other? In this regard, it is helpful to consider some incentives for cooperation between these departments.

There is an obvious need to bring the employees together, but not in an unstructured name-calling event. Rather, there should be some formal team-building exercises, and one task should be for these employees to jointly develop a listing of the difficulties between their departments, as well as to formulate and commit to a strategy to resolve them.

As a side note, some managers have food available during these types of sessions, with the theory being that employees are less likely to fight when they are being fed. This may not work in all cases, but it is definitely food for thought.

That's just grate

Q. I do not like a particular employee who reports to me. He's doing a decent job, but his personality grates on me. How do I deal with this?
P.R.

Nowhere in management is it required that you find the personality of every one of your employees to be charming. There are plenty of managers who describe some of their best employees as being terrific on the job, while adding that there is no way they could be friends. This is not a problem—it's just a fact.

Your job as a manager is not to be concerned about whether you and this employee have what it takes to become buddies. It makes far more sense to be concerned about his overall performance on the job.

At the same time, you must be aware that your dislike for this employee might spill over and contaminate your view of his work. If you continue to focus on the irritating aspects of his personality, it will just be a matter of time before aspects of his job performance will grate on you. In fact, this may be happening already as evidenced by your statement that he is doing a "decent" job. You specifically did not say that he is doing a good job—"decent" implies that you have some concern about his work. Is it based on performance or personality?

Try to step back and figure out why his personality annoys you. There is no quick formula to use, but there are a few tracks to follow. For example, perhaps he reminds you of someone you disliked from years gone by; perhaps his personality is closer to yours than you care to admit; perhaps he conflicts with some of your stereotypes; or, perhaps you feel that he is a threat to your job security. If you can get a better focus on why he annoys you, your chances of working effectively with him increase dramatically.

It is also important to remember that your best employees need not be your best friends. In fact, you may have more problems if they are.

The final shot

Q. I just gave my supervisor notice that I have accepted an offer for another job. She said she will need to give me an exit interview before I leave. She is an impossible boss and I've waited a long time for the chance to tell her off. Because I'm never coming back, should I do it?
K.M.

You need to look at what you can gain compared to what you can lose. On the gain side, if you launch a barrage of venom, you may unburden yourself of the deep stressful feelings that you've previously withheld.

However, when you start this attack, do you really think that your supervisor will surrender? She is more likely to launch a counterattack, and you will be quickly drawn into a full-blown argument. So much for stress reduction.

And things are not any better if her reaction is to surrender. By offering no rebuttal, she is telling you that she is not going to waste any more time with you. You can speak your piece, stamp your feet and wave your arms, but all you will be left with is the hollow feeling that accompanies a meaningless victory. This certainly does not reduce stress.

Although you are not coming back to this company, what you say in this interview matters immensely. It can come back to haunt you the next time you look for a job and references are taken. If your final meeting is a verbal bombardment, do not count on a positive reference, or a job offer.

If you want to quit as a winner, show that you are a class act in your exit interview. Be honest in describing what you liked and disliked about the company, and express your concerns in a factual, businesslike, and constructive manner. Your supervisor's final impression of you will be the most lasting one, and you have total control over what it will be.

The judgmental clique

Q. There is a new employee in our work group who is smart, efficient, and friendly. Most of the people I work with want nothing to do with her, but I like her. I don't want to alienate my co-workers, but I refuse to ignore her. Is there a way to reconcile this? F.D.

When a clique has decided that a smart, efficient, and friendly person must be avoided, one might wonder who should be avoiding whom.

One way to resolve this matter is through the leadership role that you play. If you are a leader in this group, there is a chance that your acceptance of the new employee will signal to the others that she is "okay." You should encourage them to spend more time with her.

If you are not one of the group leaders, the other approach is for you to meet with the leader and encourage him or her to be more supportive of the new person. When the clique's leader is receptive to a new person, so are the followers.

This situation may ultimately be reconciled through managerial action. Your manager may notice what is going on, or perhaps the new person will go to the manager and indicate that she is unable to meet the job expectations because of a lack of support from her co-workers, excluding you. If management gets involved, this clique is not likely to click for long.

Above it all

Q. One of the people we work with constantly tells us that she does not need to work at all and can do whatever she wants. Her attitude is annoying us, and we are all getting tired of listening to her. What do we do?
T.C.

The first step is to review your company manual to see if you are required to listen to the rantings of insecure and insensitive co-workers. Your willingness to subject yourself to them certainly raises your point total on the politeness scale, but it has not done much to make your job more rewarding.

Comments like hers typically serve one purpose: They are designed to give her more power and dominance over you and your fellow employees. In some confused way, she probably feels that this behavior will generate high levels of respect, influence, and prestige at work. Unfortunately for her, these actions generate the exact opposite outcome.

There is absolutely no reason why you have to listen to them. If you are in a situation where they start to emerge, simply excuse yourself and get back to work.

At the same time, you could consider doing this person a huge favor: Let her know exactly how she is being perceived by all of you. If she is unaware of her behavior, this feedback could help her, and it could also help solve the problem for you and your fellow employees. The next time she starts to expound on her lifestyle, sit down with her in private and tell her how you feel about her comments. Focus specifically on what she has said, while avoiding any kind of personal attack. Let her know that her comments are upsetting to all of you, and ask her how she would feel and what she would do if she were in your position. Wrap up the conversation with positive expectations about working together in the future.

If there is no subsequent change in her behavior, it is possible that her questionable attitude is reflected in her productivity. Maybe it's time for a chat with your department manager.

High-tech power player

Q. One of the technical people in our office keeps changing the way that our computer system operates so that no one else can do much of anything with this equipment unless she is available. She claims that she is improving the system, but because of her changes, the manual is useless. What should we do?
A.F.

This is a classical power play. Your co-worker may claim that she has made the changes to help the department, but her behavior more than likely has one objective: to give her power over you and your fellow employees. She sounds like a person with a strong need for control, and it also sounds like nothing has been done to control her.

There is a missing ingredient in all of this, namely your departmental leadership. If your manager is aware of this problem, why has he or she not taken immediate action to deal with it? And, if your department manager is not aware of it, why not?

Your first step should be to meet with the controlling co-worker. In doing so, be sure to avoid any judgmental comments about her personality, and focus your attention on the kinds of actions that may solve the problem. For example, indicate to her that you would like some steps to follow in order to operate the system when she is unavailable. If she is truly motivated to help the department, the problem should end there.

However, if you hit a glitch with her, the next step is to approach your manager. In doing so, indicate that a problem has developed that is undercutting performance and productivity. Briefly describe the situation and then present various methods to solve it. For example, there may be a need for a policy indicating that the computer systems are not to be altered without prior management approval. And, if such permission is granted, the changes must be communicated to all of the appropriate employees in writing and with formal follow-up training if necessary.

The irony in this situation is that the controlling employee is actually out of control. Unless some prompt actions are taken, her actions can shut down more than just computers.

Job deflation

Q. During the past six months, my manager has taken away more and more of the responsibilities that I enjoy, leaving me with the less interesting responsibilities. I met with him and voiced my dissatisfaction, but all he did was cut my job more. What should I do? G.D.

When your manager has made a job of reducing your job, this is a bad sign. You were correct to meet with him and let him know where you stand, and his cutting response tells you where he stands.

Expressing your dissatisfaction regarding your manager's action is only part of what you should do in this situation. Because he is still in a downsizing mode when it comes to your responsibilities, you need to meet with him again to talk about the future rather than the past.

You should meet with him to discuss where he sees the job going, and where he sees you going. Give him a clear idea of the kinds of responsibilities that are particularly satisfying to you, and let him know the specifics of what you want to be doing at work, both on a short-term and long-term basis. If there are responsibilities that you believe must remain in your job, be sure to let him know about them, as well.

Listen carefully to what he has to say during this meeting, and look carefully at what he does after it. If you find that more of your preferred responsibilities are going elsewhere, perhaps you should be going elsewhere, too.

Chapter
—12—

Complaints, Complaints, Complaints

There are some employees who do not seem to be happy unless they are unhappy. And, they seem to be most satisfied when they can sink their teeth into a good complaint. In fact, if there is nothing to complain about, they may complain about that.

These people have no qualms about burning countless hours of their own time, as well as the time of their co-workers and managers. After all, complaints cannot be developed in an instant. They take time. These employees have to find the situation, pull out whatever seems to be dissatisfying about it, structure a complaint, and then voice it countless times, even in writing if necessary.

Perhaps the greatest irony of all is that the career complainers do not realize that they are actually a source of complaint from many of their associates. When people constantly air complaints, they need to understand that the actual image they are creating is not that of the voice of the people or the conscience of the organization, but rather the voice and conscience of a jerk.

The best way for managers or associates to deal with complainers is to help them do more than complain. The complainers need to be advised to think about the source of their complaints, and then try to develop some suggestions to correct the issue at hand. Although some complainers may actually complain about being expected to do this, it is the best way for everyone to profit from those employees who have evolved into self-appointed complaint departments.

Complaints about decisions

Q. One of my employees wrote me a very irate note complaining about a couple of decisions that I made, and she concluded it with a rather nasty epithet. The decisions were essential, and I discussed them carefully with the employees they affected, including her. What is best way to deal with this?
W.K.

You have an employee in trouble and a troubled employee. She is most likely bothered by far more than the decisions you made. After all, even if your decisions were somewhere in the outrageous range, a letter filled with nastiness and name-calling is beyond outrageous.

The first step is to meet with her as soon as possible. Let her know that you are interested in hearing about her concerns and complaints now and in the future, but the hostility and nastiness are not going to do anybody any good. If she needs to vent, let her do so. Perhaps she will bring out what is truly bothering her.

Either way, ask if she can think of a better way to handle this type of situation in the future, whether in writing or in person. Be sure to let her know your specific expectations regarding her behavior. You can conclude by asking for her thoughts about the objectives, along with the kinds of steps that she can take in order to meet them. She needs to understand that there is no room for unprofessional behavior, and, unlike the old axiom, names can hurt her.

Complaints about the treatment

Q. I'm part of our company's professional staff, and one of the people we work with is always complaining about not being treated professionally by senior management. Although most of us agree that we could probably be treated better, it's not that big of a deal. How do we get her to put things into perspective?
S.L.

In every organization, there are people who look for problems, and people who look for solutions. If the problem-seekers cannot find a problem, it is just a matter of time before they create one...or become one. This tendency is part of their personality; it is part of what and who they are.

For people who are "always" complaining about the way that they are being treated, the act of complaining has become a habit. And, as is evident by the sorry state of most New Year's resolutions by mid-January, habits are difficult to break, even for people who want to do so. Importantly, your co-worker has given no indication whatsoever that she sees any need to alter her behavior.

The next time she starts to unleash some verbiage regarding the way that all of you are being treated, you and your fellow employees should sit down with her and talk about the specific actions that she regards as unprofessional treatment. The next step is to discuss any possible impact that such treatment can have on your work, responsibilities, personal growth, or professional development. The idea is to identify any specific damage that is associated with the so-called unprofessional treatment. Let her see that the managerial actions that have her up in arms can be rather harmless.

The broader objectives are to give her a more appropriate framework for analyzing this treatment, and to let her know that all of you are willing to work on plans and suggestions to deal with major managerial actions that truly undercut your professional roles.

If you find that she is spending less time on problems, and more time on solutions, you should give her some positive feedback for doing so. And, if she makes some particularly effective suggestions, you should work with her in refining them and presenting them to management. At the same time, while this approach may refocus her perspective, don't be surprised if it merely refocuses her complaints.

Complaints about staffing

Q. I am a department manager, and my employees are constantly complaining about needing more staff. But, whenever I hire new people, the present group runs them off and then starts complaining again. How do I break the cycle?
L.F.

Because high turnover among newly hired employees is not uncommon, it will be helpful to determine whether these employees are being run off or if they are just walking out. The best step to take at this point is to conduct some exit interviews with the departing employees. After all, there can be any number of issues that are pushing or pulling them from your company.

You may indeed have a clique that is behind the rush toward the exit, but there may be several other factors causing this permanent fire drill. For example, new employees may leave because of pay inequities, a mountainous workload, oppressive working conditions, an outdated orientation, prehistoric supervisory practices, tantalizing opportunities down the block.... Each of these conditions calls for different reactions from management.

If you find that your present employees are in fact giving the new hires a psychological shove out the door, there are some steps to take. Meet with the employees and tell them that you want to improve the retention of new employees, but you need their help. With this in mind, consider forming a task force of employees to develop some specific strategies and programs to reduce turnover of new hires. Be prepared for a broad range of recommendations that might include increasing their own role in recruitment and selection, a redesigned employee orientation program, or increased incentives.

The bottom line is that when employees have an increased role in designing programs to improve retention of new hires, there is an increased likelihood that they will develop effective programs, and they will have increased motivation to make them succeed.

Complaints about paperwork

Q. The employees in my department frequently complain to me about the amount of paperwork they have to complete. I tell them that the paperwork is part of their jobs, and there's not much I can do beyond that. Are there any other ways to deal with this concern?

T.T.

In a word, there's paperwork and there's paperwork. Some exists because it is essential, and some exists because it is traditional. What's really essential is for management to separate the two.

Review all of the paperwork that your employees are expected to complete. If you find any that falls into the traditional category, toss it. The next step is to let the employees know about any paperwork you have eliminated, and provide them with full information as to your findings on the remaining documentation. Let them know the function of each piece of paper that is expected of them—many employees dislike paperwork because they have no idea as to why it must be completed in the first place.

A related approach is to ask for employees' suggestions on ways to streamline the paperwork. You can meet with the employees on this matter, or you can consider forming an employee committee to review the paperwork and suggest methods to expedite it. In taking this type of step, it will be very important for you to commit at the outset to implement their suggestions wherever feasible.

In every organization, there are always a few employees who are particularly adept at handling paperwork. These employees should certainly be considered for any committee that is charged with paperwork streamlining, and it would also be helpful to consider having them lead a few training sessions where they can demonstrate their techniques. Employees tend to learn a great deal from co-workers who can model the actual behaviors that lead to success.

On a long-term basis, it will make sense to review the possibility of updating your entire information processing system and focus more on increased computerization. Many companies have found that this is the real answer to their paperwork questions.

Complaints from a constant complainer

Q. I am a regional manager, and one of the newer branch managers that reports to me complains constantly. It's gotten so bad that I don't return all of her phone calls because I don't have the time to listen to her complaints. How should I deal with her?
J.N.

By failing to return this complaining manager's phone calls, all you have really done is add another item to her laundry list of complaints. There are some strategies that can be helpful in defusing explosive complainers, but refusing to talk to them is not one.

People complain for any number of reasons, many of them legitimate. At the same time, you may be dealing with a card-carrying complainer for whom complaints are a way a life—this is the person who goes to a restaurant and complains about the quality of the food, and then adds that the portions are too small. Between these endpoints, there can be any number of reasons for excessive complaining, including a desire for more attention, guidance, structure, or control.

Your first move is to identify the reason for the complaints. The best way to do this is to meet with this manager and let her put all of her complaints on the table. You should address them one-by-one and indicate exactly what you will or will not do with them, while also providing her with specific techniques to resolve some of them herself. By looking very carefully at the quantity and quality of the complaints, and at the actions she has already taken to resolve them, you will get a much clearer idea about what motivates her complaining.

On a broader basis, it appears that she needs to have a clearer understanding of what you expect of the managers who report to you. It sounds like your approach calls for them to show a high degree of autonomy and independent decision-making. If this approach tends to generate further complaints on her part, then you are looking at a fundamental mismatch of expectations—the ultimate breeding ground for an infestation of complaints.

Complaints about questionnaires

Q. My manager has asked me to give our employees a short questionnaire every month in order to keep track of their satisfaction. I do not think this is a good idea. Does it make any sense to you?
T.E.

Unless administered properly, questionnaires that are supposed to measure satisfaction can actually decrease satisfaction. One of the best ways to annoy the troops is to oversurvey them.

The idea of keeping track of the employees' level of satisfaction on a regular basis is a good one. It is important to know how employees feel because their satisfaction can be closely related to such issues as productivity, turnover, absenteeism, and tardiness.

However, too much of a good thing is not good. You are going to find that the employees will tire of being surveyed so often, and they will quickly raise a more important question: What is management doing to correct the issues that are causing dissatisfaction? For example, if the employees are expressing dissatisfaction every month regarding the company's lack of incentive programs, and nothing is being done about this, the employees are going to become increasingly dissatisfied, not only because of the lack of incentives, but because their time is being wasted and their comments are being ignored.

If management is interested in determining whether dissatisfaction is increasing or decreasing, it makes more sense to conduct an annual survey, take specific actions to correct the issues that are raised, and then look at what is happening with productivity, absenteeism, turnover, and tardiness.

Complaints about you

Q. I am having serious problems getting along with one of the people who report to me. She has a difficult and abrasive personality, and she is always ready to complain about whatever I do. We have met with management to discuss this, but nothing has worked. What do you suggest in this type of situation?
C.W.

Your employee is overlooking an important part of her working relationship with you: The reality is that you are the manager. It sounds like you have tried to establish a cordial and supportive working relationship with this individual, but it is not happening.

This does not mean that your employee is entirely to blame. In fact, she may perceive you as a difficult and abrasive person. Either way, it is time for both of you to focus on the job that needs to be done, rather than on personality differences. You and this employee need to come to an agreement regarding the objectives, standards, and performance expectations for her position, and she should be evaluated strictly on her effectiveness in these areas.

Importantly, if her abrasiveness is interfering with her effectiveness, that should be noted in any formal assessment of her performance. When she is given feedback, it should be in terms of specific behaviors and measurable indicators of productivity, rather than in terms of general descriptors or labels. You should also provide her with some guidance regarding the kinds of steps for her to take in order to meet the established standards. She also needs to understand the reality of the consequences associated with sub-par performance.

Chapter
—13—

Securely
Dealing With
Insecurity

Although many jerk-like behaviors are designed to portray confidence, strength, and dominance, the fact that an employee feels compelled to display them merely highlights his or her underlying self-doubts.

Employees who constantly insult, degrade, or downgrade their co-workers, while spending an equal amount of time placing themselves on pedestals, are merely playing out their own insecurities. Their behavior is often disruptive, destructive, and annoying, but such outcomes are not altogether unwanted by them. In fact, they are a twisted form of control.

There is no magic formula that takes these insecure individuals and turns them into Rocks of Gibraltar, since their insecurities are part of their personalities. In fact, the Rock of Gibraltar is easier to change than a personality. At the same time, there are ways to securely deal with these individuals so that their antics and actions are less likely to rock the organization.

I have an MBA and you don't

Q. There is a person in our department who recently received his MBA, and now all we hear is how this or that issue was handled in his classes. Although he is the only MBA in the group, we are all highly educated and experienced, and we are tired of listening to this. How do we deal with him?
T.K.

It sounds like your colleague must have missed the MBA classes in behavioral science, particularly the sessions that focused on communication, team-building, and interpersonal relations. He also sounds insecure and, when in doubt, he is hiding behind this degree.

However, before taking any action to deal with him, there are a couple of questions for you and your associates to answer first. For example, is it possible that any of you may be jealous because he has an MBA and you do not? Secondly, is it possible that you can learn anything from him when he relates real-world problems to the classes that he took in the MBA program?

Depending upon your answer to these questions, you can certainly meet with him to jointly discuss the ways that all of you can work more productively together. Within such a context, you can give him some feedback regarding his specific behaviors, as well as solicit feedback from him regarding yours. This will actually be similar to the MBA classes that he may have missed.

The friendly insult

Q. Whenever I am at a meeting with my manager, he always has a couple of "friendly insults" about me in front of the others. I don't like this, but it is the only thing I don't enjoy about working with him. I don't feel like creating a problem, so I'm not sure what to do.
M.G.

There is no way that you can create a problem that already exists. In fact, it even has a title: manager. Rather than worrying about causing a problem, your focus should be on devising a strategy to correct one. It may be tempting to give your manager a good elbow every time he delivers a put-down, but there is no point to adding injury to insult.

Whether or not you recognize it, your manager is threatened by you. It does not matter if he has any real need to be concerned about the possibility of your upstaging him, he wants to make sure that this does not happen. By his little put-downs in front of an audience, he is trying to let everyone know that he is the star, and you better not outshine him.

You implied that all other aspects of your working relationship with him are positive. If this is the case, presumably you can openly express your concerns about any aspect of work to him. In this kind of working relationship, if there were something about your performance that bothered him, no doubt he would mention it to you. In turn, now that there is something about his performance that bothers you, it is fair and appropriate for you to mention it to him.

It's always important to voice your concerns about a particular behavior as close to an actual incident as possible, but this does not mean you should launch into him at the next meeting just as he delivers what he thinks is a master insult. As soon as the two of you have a chance to talk and debrief after the meeting, you should tell him what you think.

Your comments should not focus on him, but rather should be directed only at the behavior that bothers you. You should be as specific as possible, let him know your feelings about it, and tell him that you want it to stop now. If he is as good a manager as you think he is, he'll get the message.

The final insult

Q. My manager often compliments my work, but ends his comments with a little dig. This or that could have been better, or if I had only done one thing or another differently. He does this to everyone. Why can't he just say something positive and let it go at that? A.F.

His behavior is fairly typical of an insecure manager. If he lavishes praise on the troops without adding the little insults, that could mean that the employees' work is as good as his, and that is too much for him to handle. His thinking races to an even greater fear: Perhaps management will let him go and put one of his employees in his place.

In order to prevent you or anyone in the department from running ahead of him, your manager feels compelled to hook a little snag on all of your work. His unkind cuts help him feel more secure and powerful.

It may be helpful to approach him and express your concern, and even mention the many positive effects that accompany positive feedback. Unfortunately, because his behavior is more a reflection of personality than managerial skills, he is not likely to change. And, you already know what kind of comment he is going to make at the end of this discussion.

To quote the experts

Q. We have a new employee in our professional group who is always citing or quoting some study or person. There is rarely a need for this in most of our discussions. How do we tell him?
T.I.

It is ironically tempting to cite an appropriate response, such as the words of Sydney Smith (1771-1845), "What you don't know would make a great book." However, since this particular employee seems to be most comfortable in the world of citations and quotations, this may not be the way to go.

There is no particular reason why some people feel compelled to communicate in such a way that their comments need footnotes. For some, there may be underlying insecurities, and flashing this knowledge may make them appear and feel more intellectual. Others are in fact highly intellectual, and this is the way their minds work.

You are dealing with a new employee, and this may merely be part of the way that he copes with new situations. As he becomes more comfortable, there may be fewer citations.

Regardless, rather than being incited by his tendency to cite, it makes more sense for you to focus on his performance, effectiveness, and contributions to your department. It is possible that his arguably eccentric behavior may lead to increased departmental creativity. At the same time, it may be helpful to take a look at yourself and the possibility that this new employee's expertise may be making you feel a little insecure.

Flirting with insecurity

Q. I work in a bank, and some of the other women I work with claim that I flirt with the male customers. I'm friendly to all the customers, and I resent being called a flirt. How can I change this false image of me?
A.F.

The one person who knows if you are flirting is you. Deep down, the flirt always knows. If you are flirting with the customers, it's also worth noting that you are flirting with trouble. But if you can honestly say that you are not a flirt, that's the end of this issue.

In terms of dealing with the mistaken image of you, there is not much direct action to take. If it makes you feel better, you can approach the gaggle of co-workers and discuss the matter. However, don't expect them to suddenly their opinion. The problem is that you can look at your behavior and see an animated, personal, and enthusiastic approach to your customers, while the gaggle looks at the exact same behavior and sees an advanced stage of amorous banking.

The reasons for their determination that you are flirting are probably based on some wishful thinking. For example, they may be jealous of your friendly style of dealing with the customers and wish that they could do the same. Since they cannot, they redefine it as flirting. Perhaps they have actually done some flirting in the past, or secretly wish that they could be doing so now, but that's not in the cards. This draws them to the issue of flirting and causes them to see it in cases where it does not exist.

The fact is that the comments about your so-called flirting did not come from your manager, and there obviously has not been a groundswell of complaints from the customers. Just because some fellow employees have gone petty does not mean that you need to change your behavior.

Regardless of your actions, the little group would keep the flirt label pinned on you because of their own baggage. If you are not a flirt, don't focus on their image of you. It's their problem, not yours. If you want to build better work relationships, focus on some of your other co-workers who do not share the flirting fantasy.

Me first

Q. A person I work with makes himself the center of everything that's discussed. He shrugs off what we say, but we are expected to listen as he talks endlessly about himself. How do we change this?
L.N.

Your associate's behavior is typical of people who are best described as "security-challenged." They quickly dance through the motions of listening to others, while viewing every discussion as an invitation to a tale about themselves. No matter what the topic, they are always ready to pounce with, "That reminds me of when I...."

In fact, one of the real telltale signs of an egocentric is the number of times that "I" and "me" invade their conversations.

Dealing with a fellow employee who fills his speech with self-talk is a straightforward matter. If there are business issues to discuss, then you should discuss them. When "I" and "me" start to make their appearance, all you need to do is show some assertiveness and direct the conversation back to the business issue at hand, or if the discussion is about to end, you can easily excuse yourself on the basis that you have work to do.

A more basic question is why you feel you are "expected to listen" to his stories. He is a fellow employee at your job level, and you are under no formal obligation to remain riveted as he waxes eloquently about himself. Many people are concerned about being impolite in these situations, but by acting in a businesslike way, you can end a conversation without ending a working relationship. Frankly, many self-talkers are accustomed to having their stories abridged.

By letting the self-talker ramble on, you are actually sending him a message that you are interested in his tales of glory. In essence, you are rewarding the behavior, so he is even more likely to repeat it.

This means that the best way to change this situation is to change your behavior. If you are thinking about trying to change his, it is important to note that the behavior of the self-talker is a direct reflection of his personality, and it would be easier for you to change planes in mid-air. In fact, if you were to give him some friendly feedback regarding his tendency to turn every conversation into a diatribe about himself, you would soon hear, "That reminds me of when I...."

Resigned to resign

Q. One of the managers who reports to me is doing something that I find to be most annoying: Whenever he makes a mistake, he asks if he should submit his resignation. I have told him to stop, but he persists anyhow. How do I get him to stop?
M.M.

This manager's behavior has insecurity stamped all over it. Unfortunately, you cannot change the behavior of an insecure manager by issuing an order. In fact, by telling him to stop asking if he should resign, you may have actually fueled his insecurity because he is unable to follow your directive.

The first action to take is to try to determine if there is anything about your leadership style or developments in the company itself that may be exacerbating his feelings of insecurity. If there are threats of layoffs or impending downsizing, or if your style is one of those "my-way-or-the-highway" approaches, you can expect him to continue to quiver.

Although the era of making grandiose promises to employees about their future with a company has passed, there are some steps that you can take to help this manager feel more secure. For example, because insecurity can be heightened because of a lack of information about what is going on in the company, you should consider having increased communication with him about plans, changes, and developments. Let him know more about the short-term and long-term goals and the strategies to meet them, and try to give him more of an opportunity to express his ideas and suggestions. The more he knows about what is going on, the more secure he is likely to feel.

In addition, increased communication with this manager will also provide him with more of an opportunity to discuss his work with you, and this should lead to a decrease in mistakes and a further increase in his feelings of security.

At the same time, it will be important for you to continue to monitor his mistakes, particularly in terms of their magnitude, frequency, and the extent to which he is learning from them. Unless he starts to show some improvement, you may want to consider his resignation offer more carefully.

About her money

Q. One of our co-workers is constantly bragging about the money she is making in the stock market. We are all tired of hearing about it, but we don't know what to say to her. What's the best way to handle this?
N.J.

Her need to boast about her securities may well be a sign of underlying insecurities. Bragging about her stocks' new highs is seemingly giving her some new psychological highs as well.

If you cannot bear any more of her bullish comments, she needs to be told. Tell her that most of you feel she is spending too much time talking about her stocks, and many of you are bored with it. Let her know that you enjoy working with her, but surely there must be some other topics to discuss, including some that relate to the work that all of you are supposed to be doing.

It is also important to remember that as much as people may talk about their stocks when they are going up, they tend to be much quieter when they are going down. Whenever the market makes a correction, you can expect this co-worker's behavior to make a correction, too.

The other side of the coin may be to step back and consider this co-worker as a resource. If you have a cordial group of employees, you could think about forming a little investment group. This could be done during non-work hours, and there are plenty of success stories about employees and friends doing so. Perhaps all of you would actually like to have the same bragging rights as your co-worker.

About your money

Q. I am an account executive, and every month when our results are posted, one of our team members accesses and reviews everyone's monthly production from an online system. Then he walks through the office asking each of us if we met our goals, knowing full well he's met his. It's very frustrating knowing that he's doing this just to get some kind of reaction from us. What do you advise?
E.B.

There are a number of strategies to take when dealing with an employee who is about as secure as the San Andreas Fault. You are quite charitable in describing him as a team member—he may be a member of the group, but he is hardly part of the team.

Fortunately, there are some steps you can take to end his monthly ritual. The first is the honest and direct approach. The next time he marches in to supposedly inquire about your performance, level with him. You can do this on your own or with a couple of your fellow account executives. Either way, tell him that if he would like to discuss ways to improve monthly performance, you'd be most interested in doing so. At the same time, tell him that his current line of questions is counterproductive and is actually undermining his working relationship with the rest of the team.

There is an approach at the other end of the continuum that is also worth considering. You recognize that he is asking these questions in order to get a reaction from you—so this means that he will keep doing so as long as you react. In other words, as long as you reward his behavior, he will continue to repeat it. If you can basically ignore his line of questioning, the lack of reinforcement may cause him to abandon it.

One additional approach deals with the bigger picture: Is this individual supposed to be accessing your performance data? Does management regard this data as public information, or is he accessing personal information that management regards as private? This point can be mentioned to him, and if he does not get the message, then it should be mentioned to management. Management may need to check its current security measures, and may indeed wonder about other files your questioning co-worker may be accessing.

No comment

Q. I was at a holiday lunch with several people in our department, including our manager, when one person in the group made a very insulting comment about my intelligence. Everyone suddenly became quiet, but I let it go. Now I am really upset. Should I have said something to him at the time, and what do I do now?
M.P.

The only person at your holiday lunch who demonstrated a lack of intelligence was the person who insulted you. In fact, by letting it go at the time, you demonstrated a high level of restraint, self-respect, and class. Had you snapped back at this individual, all you would have done is drop to his level.

Because his comments are still turning your stomach, you should say something to him. However, you need to know at the outset that a person who is foolish enough to make that kind of a comment is also foolish enough to refuse to listen to others. Nonetheless, if it makes you feel better, you can tell him how you feel about the comment, and ask him how he would feel if he had been on the receiving end.

More importantly, keep the big picture in mind: He made a fool out of himself in front of your manager, and you demonstrated to your manager that you are a quality person. If your manager is sharp, he or she will have already spoken to this employee. After all, if your co-worker acts like this during a holiday luncheon, how does he act on a day-to-day basis? If his behavior persists, he may be a candidate for a permanent holiday.

Chapter
—14—

We Can't Go On Meeting Like This

People at virtually every level of an organization attend meetings, and many spend more time in meetings than in any other singular activity at work. The reasons for holding meetings are endless, and, unfortunately, many meetings seem endless, too.

Meetings offer excellent opportunities to creatively solve problems, develop challenging short-term and long-term objectives, formulate cutting-edge plans and strategies, and generally help an organization run more productively and effectively. At the same time, meetings also offer excellent opportunities to generate dissatisfaction, frustration, and "groupthink."

There are countless ways that jerks can turn meetings into a mess, ranging from poor timing and a questionable locale, all the way to muddled objectives, the wrong participants, and totally inappropriate leadership behavior. Rather than being worked over in meetings, there are some steps that you can take to help make meetings work.

A weekly thrashing

Q. We meet with the chief operating officer at the end of each week, and he goes around the table and tears into each of us for some problem or another that occurred during the week. The other managers let these comments roll off their backs, and they have told me to do likewise, but I can't. I do a good job and enjoy working here, but this is getting to me. What do you suggest?
A.P.

When your chief operating officer turns management meetings into management beatings, there are a few steps to consider. Unfortunately, it does not sound like your fellow managers are particularly concerned about this matter, and this eliminates the attractive option of joining ranks with them and approaching the executive as a group.

However, this does not mean that you cannot meet with the chief operating officer yourself. Because your treatment in these meetings seems to have taken you to the point that it will be hard for you to continue with the company as long as these meetings continue, you have nothing to lose by approaching him on your own.

When you meet with him, preferably at the beginning of the week, let him know how much you enjoy working for the company, and then ask him what he thinks of the meetings. Regardless of his response, ask him if he is open to any suggestions that may help make them more productive. If his response is negative, there is one question left, and it is for you alone: Can you live with these meetings? At the same time, if he replies affirmatively, propose that he put together a task force of employees to suggest ways to improve the meetings.

For example, perhaps it will be more effective to have a meeting at the beginning of the week to clarify objectives, and then have a meeting at the end of the week to review progress. And, in these latter meetings, it may be more useful for the employees to evaluate their own performance, if any evaluation at all is actually appropriate. In fact, when an objective has not been met, it makes more sense for the group to spend time figuring out ways to meet it, rather than spending time figuring out ways to melt the manager.

A real sleeper

Q. We have management meetings in the early afternoon twice a week. They are long, boring, and repetitive, and they provide about 20 minutes worth of content in two hours. My problem is that I am having a very hard time staying awake in them. Do you have any suggestions?

S.S.

Early afternoon meetings have often been regarded as the ultimate cure for insomnia. However, this does not have to be the case.

The first step is to look at your own basic energy level. If you find that you frequently run out of gas in the early afternoon, whether you are at a meeting, your desk, or a ball game, then it's time to focus on your own condition rather than on the condition of the meetings. Issues such as diet, exercise, sleeping patterns, stress, illness, and even job dissatisfaction can be playing a role here.

If you find that your energy level is more than appropriate in most other situations, and it is just these meetings that are lulling you into dreamland, there are a number of actions to consider. The best way to stay awake in these meetings is to be an active participant. This can be accomplished in many ways, such as by making a brief presentation, asking questions, responding to questions, or voicing suggestions. By becoming actively involved in the meetings, you are far more likely to stay sharp and alert in them.

Look around at your fellow managers during these meetings. If you see their heads following an erratic downward path that ends with the classical upward jolt, it is safe to assume that they are not being exactly energized by the meetings either. To the extent that this is occurring, you should meet with them to discuss some ways to enliven and streamline these meetings, and then meet with your manager to discuss your suggestions.

For example, if you really have 20 minutes of content in two hours, think about suggesting that these meetings be held on a stand-up basis, even if held more regularly. Stand-up meetings cut to the issues, keep the lines of communication open, allow for more direct involvement by the participants. And, they make sleeping a less attractive option, unless the participants are horses.

Give me a break

Q. We have a weekly meeting that should take less than an hour. It often stretches through the afternoon because of interruptions. Our boss leaves frequently for cigarette breaks, bathroom breaks, and phone calls—personal or business. The rest of us waste time talking about our weekends until he returns. I am growing increasingly resentful of these endless meetings, as they often put me behind in my work. What can I do to change this situation?
C.P.

Rather than having a meeting that is being interrupted by breaks, your situation sounds like breaks that are being interrupted by a meeting.

It is apparent that your boss's strengths are not in the area of planning, organizing, and running meetings. This is actually a double-edged problem. If he is aware that the breaks and interruptions are disruptive and dissatisfying, but he still persists in taking them, that is a bad sign. And, if he is not aware that the breaks and interruptions are disruptive and dissatisfying, that sign is even worse.

The best way to put these meetings on track is for you and some of your fellow attendees to discuss the situation with him. Let him see that the current meeting format is wasting time and generating unrest, and then add that you and your associates have some ideas to correct this.

Your suggestions can include having a draft agenda provided to all of the attendees ahead of the meeting, along with an opportunity for them to suggest additional topics that they think may be important to the group. There should be specific times allocated to the topics to be discussed, with time set aside toward the end for further discussion and questions if necessary. Barring emergencies, there should be a formal and finite time for breaks and phone calls for meetings that are scheduled to last for an hour or more.

If your boss is still resistant, you can suggest that he use this approach on a trial basis. Hopefully, he will see that your suggestions establish a framework in which meetings solve problems, rather than create them.

Monopolizing the meeting

Q. Even though our meetings are supposed to follow a tight agenda, they regularly get sidetracked by a staff member who focuses on small-picture issues that relate only to her work. If we had a strong leader, this wouldn't be a problem, but our manager allows this person to derail the direction every time. I feel frustrated that I have to sit through these irrelevant discussions. What can I say that won't make me sound as if I'm not a team player?
S.B.

A true team is open to the input, concerns, and suggestions of all the members, so if you have reservations about voicing your opinion on this matter, you are not really on a team in the first place. In addition, it would not be surprising to find that most of the people who attend these meetings are equally annoyed by your co-worker's self-oriented behavior and the lack of responsiveness from the manager. If this is the case, perhaps those two are the ones who are not team players.

Although you can discuss the situation with the small-picture employee, there is not much you can say that will cause her to step back and see the big picture. She is comfortable with her behavior in the meetings, and so is the manager.

For this situation to change, you and some of your teammates should tell the manager that you have some thoughts about improving the meetings, and then suggest a group discussion to go over the ways that meetings are now being held, along with ways to make them more productive. The gathering should conclude with a general consensus as to the way that meetings will be conducted in the future. Part of this consensus should be a commitment to keep the discussions focused on group-related matters, with individual matters being discussed in individual sessions with the manager. This type of approach makes for better meetings and better teams.

Left down and out

Q. Many people in my line of sales enter a partnership with a fellow professional. The problem is that the person I recently partnered with just got called for a big project and told me that it's better if I do not attend the first meeting. The call came because of her contacts, but I am concerned that I am going to be left out. Does this sound right to you?
M.T.

There are two sides to your question and to your partnership. On the one hand, if your partnership is based on trust, openness, and truly shared objectives, this is no problem at all. In fact, it can illustrate one of the advantages of partnerships. While you partner is at this meeting, you can be servicing present clients or doing more business development.

On the other hand, there is the issue of why your partner is telling you what is better for you to do. When an opportunity arises like the one you described, both of you should discuss and agree upon a strategy. Perhaps it makes sense for her to be the only one to attend, and perhaps it does not. But it makes no sense at all for her to unilaterally make the determination.

At this point, you should meet with her to discuss the situation and let her know the specific reasons why you believe you should attend the meeting with her. After all, by definition, a partnership means mutual cooperation to meet agreed-upon goals.

Where is everyone?

Q. It's most annoying to be expected to attend regular meetings when some of the people who really need to be there are rarely present. This makes the meetings a total waste of time. I have voiced this concern to management, and they agree with me, but then do nothing about it. Can anything be done?
M.A.

Somewhere in time, your company lost sight of the true objective of these meetings, and now seems to hold them just for the sake of holding them.

You have already taken the best step in this matter, namely discussing your concern with management. The fact that management agrees with you and then goes right on holding the same arguably useless meetings points to rigid thinking and is akin to management saying, "Yes, we agree that holding these meetings is ridiculous, and it is our unwavering intent to continue to be ridiculous."

If there is a level of management that is higher than the one you approached, a meeting with such a topsider may be worthwhile. However, if you have gone as high as you can go, or if you find that the same thinking prevails even at the most senior levels, then it is important to look at the big picture. In doing so, you will probably find many situations that parallel the thinking associated with these meetings. In a word, it does not sound like you are going to find a meeting of the minds here.

About the scheduling

Q. Our company has several branches between 50 and 100 miles from the corporate office. As branch managers, we waste many hours going to and from the office to attend meetings, sometimes three times a week. I told the corporate staff they need to schedule more of these meetings on one day, but they never do this. How do I get through to them?
C.P.

Your company gives a whole new meaning to the importance of having employees with a great deal of drive. In terms of getting through to the corporate staff, you told them that they need to schedule more of these meetings on one day. However, when you tell people what they need to do, they often react with resistance. Try using a sales approach that tailors your comments to the needs, objectives, and style of these corporate personnel.

For example, if they are financial types, you should make a thorough, detailed presentation that spells out the costs of the current scheduling and the savings associated with your approach. By letting them see that your thinking is similar to theirs, you are far more likely to influence them. Be sure to mention the value of alternatives such as teleconferences, e-mail, and faxes.

If the meeting schedule still appears to be better suited for stock car drivers than managers, one short-term option is to try to make the rides more productive, such as by listening to management tapes along the way. However, if the lack of topside responsiveness is typical of the way that branch managers are treated, perhaps it is time to focus more on the direction in which you are driving your career.

No impact whatsoever

Q. Our company has quality improvement committees, and I am on one. We spend hours discussing ways to improve things, and then we make recommendations. The problem is that management does nothing with them. I want to drop off the committee, but if I do, I am concerned about what management will think of me. What do you suggest?
W.D.

You are probably correct in assuming that management may wonder about your quality if you suddenly drop off a quality improvement committee. This is an option, but not one you should exercise yet.

You and your fellow committee members should inform management that you are now going to be working on a major problem that is causing dissatisfaction, wasting time, undermining morale, creating conflict, and undercutting topside credibility. When management asks what in the world that problem can be, tell them it is the quality improvement program.

For a company to have a truly operative quality improvement program, it is essential for management to take action on the recommendations presented by these committees. As you put together your recommendations, let management see the tangible benefits that are associated with implementing them, while also letting them see the broad range of direct and indirect costs associated with ignoring them.

You have a real opportunity to help establish a program that shines, while giving yourself an opportunity to shine as well.

Unceasingly unprepared

Q. Our committee meets regularly to evaluate project proposals, but one member always comes unprepared, and spends his presentation time slowly reading through the detail of his proposals that he clearly is looking at for the first time. The result is we waste time and have to put his proposals back on the agenda for the next meeting. What is the best way to deal with this?
E.C.

When one person regularly comes to a meeting unprepared, it actually means that there are two people whose preparation skills are rather thin. The first is obviously your associate who prefers to prepare for the meeting on your time rather than on his, and the second is whoever is leading these meetings.

It sounds as if your associate goes through this same routine at every meeting, and although the leader must be aware of the problem, the only action he or she takes is to table your unprepared associate's proposals to the next meeting. This outcome apparently does not upset or punish this associate, so there is no reason for him to change.

If you and some of your colleagues have a decent working relationship with this individual, you can approach him and indicate that his actions are wasting everybody's time, and all of you would be most appreciative if he would prepare for these meetings, adding that you are willing to help if he would like.

If you do not have this kind of relationship with him, or if you get nowhere in your discussion with him, you should review the situation with the leader of the meetings. If this person knows anything about management, he or she will take swift action. However, if this person is not prepared to act like a leader, then you should prepare yourselves to discuss the matter at a higher level.

Round 'em up

Q. I'm responsible for running our departmental meetings, but I feel like I'm trying to herd sheep! I have to round up everyone or the meeting will never start. I may get most of the attendees in the meeting room, but as I try to corral the last one, a couple of others wander off to get coffee or make a phone call. The meetings are regularly delayed by at least a half-hour because of this wayward "flock." What can I do?

B.S.

Before focusing on this disrespectful flock, look first at the shepherd. If you have to round up and corral the employees every time you hold these meetings, it sounds like you need to give the group some serious feedback regarding the necessity of attending these meetings on time, as well as serious feedback regarding the sanctions associated with failure to do so.

Look also at the content, organization, and usefulness of these meetings, and whether they are being held at the best time and place. Having properly placed meetings that are truly productive can have a definite impact on the attendance and the attendees. You should also consider soliciting the employees' suggestions regarding ways to improve these meetings.

At the same time, the fact is that these are departmental meetings, and everyone is expected to attend on time. Although the employees may view them as an opportunity to engage in some sort of power play with you, they need to understand that employees who engage in sheepish behavior can get sheared.

Punish the participants

Q. Our company has a mission statement that, among other things, encourages employee ideas. I had a terrific idea that I presented at an open meeting with several members of top management. One of them, who is not my manager, tore my idea apart and left me standing like a fool. I am upset, and I still think my idea would work. What should I do?

B.D.

Mission statements run the gamut from being an accurate depiction of the philosophy, culture, and objectives of an organization, all the way to being nothing more than something to occupy wall space. The fact that a top manager left you standing like a fool actually tells you where your company stands.

Equally troubling is the fact that no one else from management, including your own manager, approached you to indicate that there may be some steps for you to take if you want to develop your idea further. Nonetheless, it sounds like you are not going to be satisfied unless you go further with it.

As a result, you should consider doing some homework and putting together a summary that demonstrates how the idea will work, and how it will benefit the company. You should present the summary to your manager and ask if it can be implemented at least on a trial basis in your department, adding that if the results are anything short of outstanding, it can be scrapped.

Unfortunately, based on what you have already experienced, you may hit a wall. This is typical of a company whose mission statement is actually a submission statement.

Chapter
—15—

Training in Action vs. Training Inaction

Investing in employee training and education is critically important in today's competitive marketplace. When companies fall behind in the development of their human resources, it is not surprising to find them falling behind in countless other ways as well. An investment in employee development not only strengthens the overall company, it also strengthens individual employee motivation, involvement, and commitment.

At the same time, the area of employee development has not escaped the curse of the jerks. They can be found designing, selling, conducting, implementing, and evaluating programs, as well as insisting on some programs and resisting others. This has led to numerous educational programs that have useless content, simplistic approaches, marginal instructors, canned answers, no practice opportunities, no feedback, and no applicability whatsoever to the job.

And, even if the employees are fortunate enough to participate in a highly effective program, there can be jerks waiting on
the job to prevent any new insights or approaches from being
implemented.

The fact is that educational programs offer an opportunity to
generate a monumental array of problems. Fortunately, these programs also offer an opportunity to generate a monumental array of
solutions, particularly for those who know how to separate programs that work from programs with jerks.

The emperor's training program

Q. Our company has an in-house educational program for managers,
and I just completed it. Before I went, everyone told me that the
program is fantastic. I thought the whole thing was simplistic,
outdated, and useless. The question is, because everyone thinks it
is so great, should I say anything or just forget about it?
H.S.

If you truly believe that this educational program is anything
but educational, the real question is not if you should say something, but what you should say. For example, if you simply say the
program is useless, all you will do is raise questions about your
usefulness.

You should initially approach the individuals who conducted
the program, but do not hit them with a barrage of criticism.
Rather, you should indicate that you have some questions about
the information provided in the program. Then present very specific pieces of information that clearly support your beliefs regarding the utility of the program, and ask how the information
presented in the program fits with the facts that you have presented. The idea is that you are not trying to teach the training
specialists anything; rather, you are just trying to learn.

If your comments are ignored, you should consider approaching
senior management in the same way. If your comments are again
ignored, you can probably assume that these managers spent too
much time in that educational program. Either way, from the educational standpoint, you are about to have a real learning experience.

The return of the canned program

Q. Most of the people in my department attended a boring, canned training program put on by an outside firm a couple of months ago, and we all rated it as being poor. Now the same firm is coming back to do more training. None of us want to attend, and we have told this to our manager. She says that it is out of her hands. What should we do?

M.C.

Training programs are expensive, and most companies do not like to see how much money they can spend in order to aggravate their employees. Because you and your fellow employees gave the program an unsatisfactory evaluation on the last round, there are basically three possible scenarios.

The first is that the training company took your evaluations to heart and made some major improvements. The second is that the training company filed your comments and is going to serve another canned program. And, the third is that the training company has a tight relationship with your company, and your comments had less weight than helium.

Because your manager has indicated that the matter is out of her hands—a reaction indicating that she could actually profit from some managerial training—you and your associates should meet with whoever is handling this matter and discuss your concerns. You might learn more from this person's reaction than from any training program.

Good stuff, but not here

Q. My company sent me to a training program, and when I returned I was going to implement some new techniques about managing different personality types. When I told my manager, he reacted very negatively and said there is no time for any of that. I think I can be more effective if I at least try to apply what I learned. How should I go about doing this?

H.S.

Considering that you went to a seminar that dealt with personality types at work, you should have applied some of what you learned when you approached your manager. After all, it sounds like he could score well above average when it comes to being hostile-aggressive, over-controlling, insecure, or rigid.

One of the real problems with many training programs goes back to a buzzword called "transference." A training program may be regarded as excellent by all educational standards, but unless it truly fits into the trainee's organization, the program is doomed to failure. Your manager is a roadblock that is preventing everything you learned from transferring into your job.

However, it does not have to be this way. Part of the problem is that you approached him with a "done deal." A better approach is to meet with him, share your newly acquired expertise with him, and then discuss the ways that both of you can implement some of the new strategies, at least on a trial basis.

One caveat: Be careful about locking personality labels on those around you. People are complex, and by labeling them, you may find that there can be some unflattering labels pasted on you.

The trainer needs training

Q. Our company brought in an outside trainer who kept singling me out with questions and comments during the all-day session, and this made me uncomfortable and embarrassed. He jokingly apologized at the end and said it was all in fun, but it wasn't. I didn't say anything because I did not want to make a scene or get even more attention. What do you suggest in this situation?
V.S.

The first suggestion should be to send this so-called trainer back to obedience school so that he can learn more about dealing with people.

In this type of situation, the best step is to approach the trainer during one of the breaks and tell him in a businesslike way that you do not appreciate being singled out. Let him know that his treatment is making you uncomfortable, and then tell him that it must stop.

In addition, at the end of these programs, there is often an opportunity to review quality and effectiveness. Ideally, these written comments go to management. This is an opportunity to let the top-siders know that this trainer spent too much time on you and too little time on the topic at hand.

However, because there is a possibility that your comments may never get to management, you should also go directly to your manager and express your dissatisfaction with the trainer's be-havior. There is a long list of reasons why companies spend money training their employees, but increasing the level of dissatisfaction, humiliation, and unrest is not on it.

When the guru goofs

Q. I try to keep current on trends in management, and I just read an article by some guru, and he said that it is important for managers to set goals for employees. I thought employees were supposed to play a role in goal-setting. Can you clarify this?
M.C.

As a manager, you will rue the day you follow that guru. On the one hand, he is correct in his view of the importance of goals at work. Goals have been consistently found to have a positive impact on motivation, productivity, and satisfaction.

However, when goals are unilaterally dumped on employees, they can have the exact opposite impact. In such cases, employees feel ignored, interchangeable, and somewhat useless. If the goal of management is to generate employee resistance and resentment, this is an excellent way to do it.

It makes more sense for an organization to have clearly defined overall goals, complete with priorities, performance expectations, benchmark dates, and measurement standards, and for managers to work with their employees to jointly establish strategies that will help each individual meet his or her objectives while simulta-neously linking them with the organization's objectives.

Any guru worth his or her salt (and fees) emphasizes the im-portance of treating employees with respect and trust. Setting goals for the employees tends to neutralize rather than empower employees, and that's definitely not guru-worthy.

Mentor or tormentor

Q. When I joined this company, a person was assigned to be my mentor, but he is always too busy to help me. The last few times that I approached him, he was rather nasty. I don't want to cause problems, but I need more guidance in this job. What is the best way to deal with him?
M.S.

When a mentor acts like a tormentor, the best first step is to continue to try to work with him. However, instead of approaching him and asking a number of questions, confine yourself to one key question: When are the best times to meet?

If he is willing to set some appointments and keep them, then you can start with your most important questions and deal with lesser questions over time. With increased contact and familiarity, your mentor will get to know you on an individual basis and may be less likely to treat you so hastily in the future.

However, if you find that your mentor either refuses to make appointments or cancels them, your next step is to approach your manager and explain the situation. You should not trash the mentor during this discussion, but focus instead on your desire to learn and grow and the fact that your mentor is too busy to provide much guidance at this time. Tell your manager that you would appreciate any help that he or she could provide in this matter.

The action that your manager takes will give you a clear indicator as to whether the company regards employee development as a fact or a fad.

Inertia vs. initiative

Q. One of the people who reports to me has been with our company for several years, but she has done nothing to upgrade her skills or expertise recently, even though we provide considerable encouragement in this area. She is steady, reliable, and well-liked, and I am uncertain as to the best way to deal with her.
W.D.

It is perfectly fine to have an employee is who steady, reliable, and well-liked, but somewhere in the list of descriptors should be words like productive, industrious, and tenacious. Otherwise, you could just as easily be describing the family pet.

There are two clear sides to this situation. On the one hand, when an employee has not made an effort to upgrade his or her skills, it is easy to lay the blame at the employer's doorstep. An employee can question the employer's commitment in this area if the company provides minimal training or has almost invisible educational benefits. This means that you should carefully look at the extent to which your company truly supports employee growth and development.

At the same time, even if your company is woefully deficient in this area, employees who are motivated to enhance their expertise can act on their own in order to do so. In fact, employees who believe that it is the employer's responsibility to educate them may find that the most important lesson they learn is that they are ultimately responsible for their own education.

The best step at this point is to review this person's performance and note areas in which specific problems could have been avoided by increased education. The next step is to meet with her, go over the performance problems, discuss the areas in which she needs to upgrade her knowledge and skill base, and jointly establish some educational objectives and a plan of action to meet them.

Now hear this

Q. My manager just returned from a week-long seminar, and now he is using all sorts of new jargon and contrived speech patterns when communicating with us. It's driving us crazy. Things were not going so badly before, and we don't know what to do now. S.G.

Your manager literally and figuratively bought the words and wisdom of the seminar leader. He spent a week seeing and hearing the marvels of his newly acquired communication skills, and now he is ready to apply them in his department. The problem is that the department is not ready for him.

It is most uplifting to attend a seminar and come back with some visible and measurable skills that can be instantly applied to a department. At the same time, although various new technical skills can be plugged in without too much disruption, new interpersonal skills are not as easy to implement. They worked well in the week-long seminar where everyone was using them, but they can have a Martian-like quality when brought back to one's own department.

If your manager is intent on applying his newly learned communication skills, the first and ironic step that he needs to take is to communicate with all of you about them. In failing to do so, all he has succeeded in doing is to unilaterally introduce a key change in the department. Your resistance is the normal and typical employee reaction.

Before allowing his new approach to generate further distress for you and your fellow employees, sit down with him and ask for more information about this new communication style. Many organizations actually expect managers who return from seminars to conduct their own mini-seminar within the company in order to bring all of the employees up-to-speed on the newly acquired knowledge. You should ask him for such a session.

At the same time, presumably you have some degree of understanding of your manager. Is he the kind of person who jumps from one managerial fad to another, only to leave his career path strewn with discarded buzzwords, modalities, and systems over the years? If so, you can sit patiently because this new approach shall pass. At the same time, if he is a cautious, reflective, and deliberative manager, your career path is about to have some entirely new road signs.

On-the-job-training...by a subordinate

Q. I work for a great manager who often asks me to proofread his writing, give him suggestions, and correct his mistakes. The problem is that his writing is terrible. His punctuation is awful, his sentence structure is wrong, and, his grammar is worse. What should I do?
K.W.

Your manager has looked at himself and the department and figured that it is the right thing to turn to you for "the write thing." By asking you to proof and correct his work, he is sending a message of confidence in your writing skills and lack of confidence in his. This may actually be one of the clearer messages that he has sent recently.

Managers are constantly advised to treat their employees as valuable resources. That is exactly what yours is doing.

Although managers are often expected to coach their employees, many understand that there are some areas in which their employees can actually coach them. They are constantly on the lookout for sources to help them learn and grow. Your manager regards you as one of those sources. This means that your issue is not focused on what to do; rather, the issue is how to do it. Before you put your pen to anything your manager has written, the first step is to sit down with him and clarify exactly what you are expected to do when reviewing and correcting his writing.

It will then be important for both of you to agree to follow-up meetings to discuss the revisions you make. One purpose of these meetings is to place your corrections in a constructive context—your manager needs to see that although you may be trashing his writing, you are not trashing him. In addition, these meetings will give you an opportunity to teach him how to be a better writer.

Don't forget that your manager writes your performance evaluation. It would be nice if he had some positive things to say, and even nicer if he could put them into sentences that make sense.

All of this comes with one caveat: It is fine for your corrections and suggestions to be used by your manager, but keep your eyes open and make sure that you are not being used.

The quick test

Q. At a recent management seminar I took some kind of a quick test. I was told that the results say I am too accommodating in my leadership style, and that I need to focus more on the task to be done. I don't think this is true, and I am upset to be labeled like this. What do you think?
K.W.

The best thing that can be said about most quick management tests is that they are quick. In terms of providing accurate, validated, and truly meaningful information, many tend to fall into the category of parlor game. They work very well as icebreakers, but they do not break new ground in management.

One problem is that these tests tend to boil all of management down to roughly a half-dozen catchy traits. Unfortunately, management is not a handful of sound bites that apply universally across all organizations. In fact, traits and styles that work well in one organization, such as being innovative or creative, may set up a manager for failure in another organization where such characteristics are viewed as rebelliousness or insubordination.

Whenever people fill out forced-choice tests about themselves, a couple of additional problems emerge. In the first place, there are times when neither option applies, but one must be selected. For example, when asked if you are more likely to insist on having everything done your way or to berate an employee in front of his or her peers, many managers believe that neither choice fits, but they must pick one anyhow. Conclusions drawn from responses to questions like this are actually inconclusive.

In addition, when people fill out these types of questionnaires on themselves, their perceptions about their own behavior can be very inaccurate, with the toughest of taskmasters mistakenly seeing themselves as kindly facilitators. And further, because the results of these tests are discussed in front of a group, some managers willfully steer their responses to look better.

There are some excellent instruments in this area, but they are not particularly quick. Often they call for you to complete a well-designed management questionnaire, and for your manager and subordinates to complete a similar one about you. The results are compared and contrasted, and a very productive discussion can follow.

The feedback you received came from extremely limited data, and, as a result, it should be given extremely limited credence.

Chapter
—16—

Dollars, Sense, and Incentives

Money can be a very powerful motivator, and many studies today are revealing that it is a critical factor in understanding turnover. However, there are jerks at work who can make all sorts of errors that undercut the positive outcomes that money or incentives can bring.

One destructive force is an inequitable or inconsistent reward system, such as one that pays newer employees more than the experienced long-termers. This practice alone creates dissension, dissatisfaction, resentment, hostility, vindictiveness, absenteeism, and turnover. Other destructive approaches include excessive emphasis on pay secrecy, outdated and outmoded incentive programs, minimal links between pay and performance, arbitrary pay-related decisions, and minimal understanding of the role of incentives.

When it comes to pay and incentives, it pays to know what to do when the jerks are pulling the purse strings.

Paying for inequitable pay

Q. I work for a major financial institution that hires new employees at a higher base salary than existing employees. I love working here, but the inequity is demotivating. What can I do?
J.M.

If a company is looking for a way to spend money in order to aggravate the employees, pay inequity is the way to go. Countless studies have found that employees may be relatively satisfied with their pay until they learn that some co-workers are being paid more for doing essentially the same work.

However, it is important for you to first address the possibility that the newly hired employees may have more experience, education, or expertise than the present staff, and the pay differential may actually be due to a skill differential. If this is the case, the real focus is for you to put together a plan to upgrade your skills.

At the same time, if you find that the only factor that differentiates pay rates among the employees in the same job and geographical area is the date of hire, you are more than likely working for a firm that has a pay system that is out of date and out of whack.

The best step is to discuss this dissatisfying development with management. Most managers realize that dissatisfaction is often a step away from turnover, and turnover is far more costly than salary adjustments. You indicated that you love working for this company, and now you are about to learn more about the depth of the company's feelings toward you.

This is no prize

Q. Our company put on a little contest and I won. The prize was not a big deal, but I never got it. When I went to the manager, he said he'd get around to it, but he never has. I don't want to make an issue out of this, but I'm upset. What do you suggest I do?
S.S.

When companies put on a little contest, only to ignore the little rules, it is a sign of management with little skills. The larger question in your situation is whether this type of behavior is extremely rare, or whether it is yet another example of management's belief that commitments also mean little.

If the delay in presenting you with your prize is an aberration, you can certainly go back to your manager and mention that you are suffering from prize deprivation and would like your just reward. Be sure to pick a time when he is not extremely busy.

However, if it is typical of your manager to conveniently forget about your prize, you can still approach him and tell him that you would like the prize, express your concern over what happened, and then ask him what he would do if he were in your situation. Then follow his advice. You always have the option of approaching his manager, but the real question is whether this issue is worth it.

Many companies have found that contests can be a great source of improved satisfaction, motivation, and even productivity. However, if handled with the least bit of inequity, they can be a greater source of distrust, distress, and dissatisfaction. And, this latter outcome is virtually guaranteed when the manager is no prize.

Pay secrecy does not pay

Q. We provide our employees with competitive pay, but I insist they do not discuss it, and they can be disciplined for doing so. But this has not stopped them. Today an employee marched in and listed all of the employees who are making more, by how much, and said he deserves more. I re-explained the policy and ended the meeting. How do I prevent this?
A.T.

It is never a good sign when employees march into your office. One way to prevent this "march madness" concerning pay inequities is to have an equitable pay system. Although your pay levels are competitive, the employees will not be satisfied with their pay unless they think it is fair. In your situation, if equally qualified employees are being paid different amounts for no apparent reason, there will be dissatisfaction.

In most organizations today, pay secrecy is an oxymoron. As long as employees are paid, they are going to talk about what they make. If pay levels are shrouded in secrecy, employees are still going to talk about what they make, only this time the numbers will be inflated.

If there is a trend in this area, it is a movement toward open-book management in which employees are given considerable information regarding financial issues and developments in their companies. If you maintain equitable and competitive pay levels, the employees will know, and they will find more important topics to discuss, such as their work.

A little consistency here

Q. Throughout last year, our company was in a cost-cutting mode, and we all worked extremely hard to make our numbers. That's why we were shocked by the extravagance of the year-end party. As a manager, how do I keep my employees focused on cost reduction after the company does something like this?
C.J.

It can be hard to maintain the company's party line on cost cutting when the company party ignores the bottom line altogether. At the same time, when a company gives a party that seems to be an inappropriate ending to the story that has been told during the year, it is best to remember that companies have these types of events for all sorts of reasons, from the sublime to the ridiculous.

For example, some topsiders regard this type of party as a way to provide the employees with a major thank-you for their hard work during the year. In other cases, management views this type of party as a tradition, and there is concern as to what the employees would think if it were scaled down.

The best step is for you to have a clear understanding of the rationale behind your company's party, and for you to communicate it to your employees. You can certainly add your opinion, and even indicate that you will check into the possibility of having more employee involvement in planning any such event for the coming year.

Having taken this step, the party is history. Your employees now need to focus on the future, or they can run the risk of being history, too.

The mouthpiece

Q. I am a newly hired marketing professional who reports to the president. Recently, I discovered that a person who has access to the employees' salaries has shared mine with others in the office. The company does not pay well, but I am paid very well because of my specific experience. There is resentment from this person and her friends, and she does not speak to me unless she has to, and then she is defensive and rude. I can't work like this. Should I bring this matter up with my boss or continue to try to resolve this directly with her?
V.W.

When you work with someone who thinks the phrase, "show me the money," means that she is supposed to show everyone your money, there are two key steps to take:

The first is to continue to deal directly with her. However, your focus should not be on her self-appointed role as corporate monetary mouthpiece. If you dwell on this, she will flip into a denial mode, and the discussion will go nowhere.

The best approach is to focus on specific instances in which she was defensive and rude. Tell her what you think about this behavior, and then present some possible ways in which the two of you can work better together. Finally, let her know about the kinds of actions you will take if the problems persist.

If she does not get the message, it's time for the second step: a meeting with your boss, the president. The company is paying a lot of money for your expertise, and the more time you have to spend with uncooperative, defensive, and rude employees, the less time is available for what you are supposed to be doing. This does not make company presidents happy.

On a broader basis, many corporate topsiders recognize that pay secrecy is outmoded. When a senior level marketing person is brought in at a high salary, it can be argued that this sends many positive messages about the company's values, standards, opportunities, and objectives. If such pay practices are causing problems for a particular person, it is apparent that the particular person is the problem.

Rejecting the referral

Q. We have an employee referral program that gives the employees cash if they refer someone to us and that person is hired and remains on the job for 90 days. One of our best employees referred his closest friend, and, after interviewing him, we have no interest in hiring him. But, we do not want to upset our strong employee. How should we deal with this?

V.S.

Just because this job applicant is close friends with one of your best employees does not mean that he has a "wild card" that automatically entitles him to instant employment. If he did not have the knowledge, skills, abilities, and other factors necessary to succeed on the job, that is all there is to this matter.

It should be noted that if the applicant informs his friend that he was treated well during the selection process, that should help diminish the likelihood of the applicant becoming upset, as well as help diminish the likelihood of your strong employee becoming upset.

At this point, you should thank your employee for referring this individual and encourage him to continue to refer others in the future. The employees need to understand at the outset that all referred applicants will be given careful consideration, and those who are excellent will be given a job offer.

A disincentive program

Q. Our company gives incentives and awards to employees in other departments, but ours is overlooked. We talked to our manager about this, and he said there is nothing he can do because our work is not set up this way. What should we do?

C.A.

Your manager may indeed lack the power to do anything about these incentives for you and your fellow employees, or he may lack the initiative or skills to do so.

There are ways for companies to provide employees in any job with opportunities to earn incentives and awards. Whether on an individual, group, departmental, or company-wide basis, each employee can participate in some sort of reward program.

Depending on your responsibilities, there can be an array of incentives associated with quality, service, productivity, attendance, work beyond the call of duty, and any other number of positive behaviors. You should do some homework and put together some suggestions as to the best way to set up such a program in your department.

Your next step is to meet with your manager again and show him your ideas. Be sure to ask for his input, and then indicate that you would like him to take the proposal to senior management. If he still says there is nothing he can do, believe him. Take the proposal to management yourself.

As a side note, some companies provide cash bonuses to their employees based on the usefulness of their suggestions. There are several reasons for you to suggest such a system in your proposal.

It's about time

Q. Our company recently sent clocks to every employee, and there are more than 100 of us. It was supposed to be a way to say thank-you for our hard work, but I don't think a clock says that at all. What do you think of this as a means of recognition?
P.D.

Gifts to all of the employees can generate all sorts of reactions, from appreciation to aggravation. Interestingly enough, employee reaction tends to be caused less by the gift itself, and more by whatever else may be going on in the company at the time.

For example, in situations where a company treats employees with low levels of respect or trust, uses harsh supervisory practices, or has inequitable pay practices, most employees are not going to be particularly enthralled with any gifts. In this context, gifts are typically viewed as a form of manipulation, a waste of money, or a useless trinket.

At the same time, in companies that have truly progressive management and up-to-date policies and programs, the employees recognize that top management truly values them as resources, and any form of recognition is appreciated.

Now, if you are in the former type of company, it is not surprising that you do not have the time of day for a gift clock. However, if you are in the more progressive type of company and still feel that a clock is a poor form of recognition, the time has arrived for you to recognize the broad range of benefits associated with working for your present employer.

A basic suggestion

Q. Management is always telling us that our suggestions are important and that we can get cash awards if they are implemented. I have submitted three or four and I have not heard one thing. When I told my manager, he said that my suggestions could not be used, but I should submit more. What do you think?
S.T.

You should submit one more suggestion to management: Trash the present program and put in a real one. A real suggestion program provides employees with feedback on each of their suggestions, whether terrific or ridiculous.

A program that only provides feedback and awards to the select few whose ideas are implemented is virtually guaranteed to increase dissatisfaction, frustration, annoyance, and embarrassment for the much larger number of employees whose suggestions are rejected.

Even if your suggestions were beyond ridiculous, management should have thanked you for submitting them, given you some guidance as to ways to help make them work, and encouraged you to resubmit them as well as to submit more. Management needs to remember that some of the most creative ideas are initially regarded as beyond ridiculous.

Less-than-inventive incentives

Q. We introduced an incentive program for safety, quality, and service that puts the employees in drawings for prizes if they perform well. The employees don't seem to care much about the program, and we have seen no significant changes in their performance. What happened?
R.M.

When an employee incentive program does not incentivize, it is time for a second look at the program and the employees.

Drawings sound like fun, but the problem is that they do not consistently reward the employee for excellence in performance, but rather place the employee in a game of chance in which he or she may or may not be rewarded. If an employee works hard and gets into the drawing a couple of times and does not win, that employee may think twice about putting forth the effort needed to get into the drawing again.

If you are going to stay with the drawings, you should also consider giving an automatic win to any employee who has reached them a certain number of times but has not yet won.

Looking specifically at the employees, the best way to develop an incentive program is with their input. After all, if you really want to know more about what motivates them, ask them. This does not mean that the entire program must be designed around their suggestions, but you certainly stand a better chance of having a successful program if they have helped create it. In terms of employee incentives, having this type of input opportunity has been found to be motivational in and of itself.

There is nothing wrong with having drawings as part of an incentive program, but if they are the core of the program, the employees can easily be drawn away.

Chapter
—17—

All in
the Family
Business

There are millions of family businesses scattered across the United States, and they range literally from mom-and-pop operations to Fortune 500 corporations. Their most common problems are based upon whether they are a family *business* or a *family* business. Those that keep the focus on business tend to encounter fewer of the classical family business problems. As a rule, they strive to make decisions in a professional, equitable, and business-like way for all of the employees.

Those that focus primarily on the family side of the equation tend to face a constant wave of conflict, complaints, chaos, and crises. Decisions concerning hiring, firing, transfers, promotions, assignments, and the like are much tougher because there are emotionally charged family considerations that cloud the business considerations.

Also in the *family* business, there is the issue of role conflicts. For example, although the owner's son is supposed to be a vice president, the owner-father may still treat him as his baby boy. This can lead to the use of kid gloves and condescending treatment, or it can lead to an emotional outburst that no other employee would ever have to face. Either way, the confusion of roles creates problems for everybody.

All of this is further compounded by the fact that just about every family has its jerks, and they can be found at virtually any level in the family business. The problems that they create are serious business, and the best way to deal with these people is to be serious and businesslike.

That son of a boss

Q. The owner of our company recently hired his son to work here in a very senior position. His background in this field is marginal, and he has an abrasive personality. Many of us have been here a long time, and the company always had a family-like atmosphere, but we are thinking of leaving because of him. What should we do now?
S.F.

It is ironic that a company can have a family atmosphere until a family member is hired. The fact is that a family business needs to be based on business, rather than on family. When these priorities are reversed, the whole company can move in reverse.

If you are certain that the owner's son lacks the wherewithal to handle the job, and that his abrasiveness is not a reaction to some resentment by you and your fellow employees, your best option is to meet with the owner.

Tell him that placing his son in this position is grossly unfair...to his son. It is important for the owner to see that by putting him in a job far over his head, his son is extremely likely to fail. In fact, his son's abrasiveness may already be a reflection of his uncertainty in the job.

You should suggest some positions that seem to be more appropriate for his son, whether within the company or on the outside. The owner is about to let you know the role of family and business in this family business, and this will help you figure out what to do from here.

Ins and outs with in-laws

Q. I hired my brother-in-law for a management position not long ago, and it's apparent already that he is failing. However, I have real concerns about the impact on our family if I terminate him. What do you suggest?
B.D.

The most important thing to keep in mind is that there is a real difference between a family tree and an organization chart. The more that you let the former influence the corporate ladder, the less effective you and your company will be.

If any employee is sinking on the job, you need to respond in a businesslike way. This means that the first step is to sit down with your brother-in-law, review his performance, and see if there is anything that you can do in terms of increased guidance, training, follow-up, or support. He needs to know precisely how he is doing, and the two of you should jointly develop plans and objectives to correct any problem areas. It is important for your brother-in-law to understand the upside potential associated with improved performance, along with the consequences associated with continued marginal work.

As uncomfortable as you are dealing with a relative whose performance is not up to par, it is important to remember he is probably feeling doubly bad not only because of the failure, but because of the fact that he is failing in your eyes. The family matter weighs heavily on him, and he is probably sensing high levels of stress and embarrassment. In fact, he is probably more concerned than you about the impact of his performance on the family.

As is a good idea with any employee, it makes sense to see if there is a more appropriate position for him within the company. Perhaps he will be more squarely pegged in another hole.

However, if there is nothing available, and you have given him every fair and agreed-upon opportunity to succeed, he can be terminated...but not exterminated. This means that you do not just show him the door. Rather, the most equitable and constructive method is to use an outplacement approach where he is given guidance and support in understanding his own strengths and skills and in locating a more suitable position. As for the family reaction, they will probably be relieved that he has been relieved.

Family feud

Q. I work for a relative and have been clashing with her and her husband over differences in opinion. I am very opinionated, and that often puts me in trouble. We see each other outside of work, and the situation has negatively affected my work life and personal life. I don't know what to do.
A.P.

When having clashes with relatives at work, the first step is relatively easy. The kind of conflict that you are describing is symptomatic of a breakdown in communication. Hence, the best approach is to meet with both of these individuals to discuss the sources of any key differences of opinion, as well as to jointly develop some strategies to resolve them in the future.

One typical problem of family businesses is the confusion of roles, as family matters often get mixed into business matters. When you meet with these relatives, it will be important to keep the discussion businesslike and professional, just as if you were dealing with management from another company. Over the longer term, if you spend less time on your relatives at work and more time on your work, you will most likely find that you are also spending less time in conflict.

Admitting that you are very opinionated is very important. Your recognition and expression of this aspect of your behavior is a solid step toward becoming a better listener. And, if you open your discussion with a comment about your being overly opinionated, you will be making a statement with which your relatives can only agree, and one of the most effective ways to open any meeting is to have others nodding in agreement.

Oh, brother

Q. My older brother runs our family business, and I report to him. We are very different personalities. He is very detail-minded, and I am more of a free spirit. The problem is that he treats me like a child. How do I get him to change?
D.B.

Regardless of personality differences, there are often difficulties reporting to big brother. After all, he spent years being bigger, stronger, and wiser than you, and it may be hard for him to recognize that you have grown up.

However, one important question is whether you actually have grown up. By describing yourself as a free spirit, you may be saying that you are not totally in step with corporate demands, commitments, and responsibilities, as spontaneity is the hallmark of your life. Before looking at your brother's behavior, you need to take an honest look at yours.

The issue is whether your being free-spirited is a help or hindrance in terms of the operations and success of the company. If you are in a tightly defined position that calls for structured thinking, you may be having some difficulties getting your work done. To the extent that this is occurring, your brother's treatment may be more a reflection of your job performance than his sibling performance.

As the corporate free spirit, you are probably best suited for a job that provides you with autonomy, performance-based rewards, variety, and a good deal of people contact. Although this is not an ironclad rule, it makes more sense to have a free-spirited sales and marketing department than a free-spirited accounting department.

Assuming your performance is up to par, keep in mind that you are not going to change your brother. The best step is to meet with him and show him specific examples of situations where he treated you like a child. Indicate that you certainly do not want favorable treatment because of your brotherly relationship, but unfavorable treatment is not acceptable, either. Give him some specific suggestions regarding more businesslike actions that he could have taken, and show him why it would make good business sense for him to do so in the future.

Off the chart

Q. The company owner's wife works here in an ill-defined managerial
position. She is not trained as a manager, but is a big know-it-all
who tells everyone what to do. How do we deal with her?
C.T.

The best way to deal with her is from afar. Many companies
have employees who seem to function as little more than walking
mines. You don't want to step on one, and you can get hurt even if
you go near them. As long as you are not reporting to this person,
try to have minimal contact with her.

Unfortunately, people in her position tend to seek out situations over which to exercise their "authority." When this occurs, the
best approach is to deal with her in a friendly, professional, and
businesslike style. If she has a self-serving barrage of questions
and answers, refer her to your manager.

The biggest mistake is thinking you can win an argument with
her. Putting aside the fact that she is the owner's wife, it is all but
impossible to prevail with any know-it-all. Bona-fide know-it-alls
will never concede that you are right, and they can drag out a disagreement with more tenacity than a 200-pound marlin. Even if
you score every single point in the debate, you will never see her
wave the surrender flag.

If, by some miracle, you do prevail, one major outcome is that
you will have succeeded in browbeating the owner's wife. You may
want to think twice about what you are really winning here.

If she is disruptive to your department, you and your fellow
employees should consider two possible approaches: The first is to
meet with your manager and point out the specific ways in which
individual and departmental performance has suffered as a result
of her intervention, and ask your manager to help deal with her. At
the very least, your manager needs to agree to be the key person in
your department to have contact with her.

Secondly, take a careful look at the owner. Is he the type of person who can be approached on a matter like this, or is such a
meeting nothing but a shortcut to the exit ramp? If he is approachable, the focus should not be a tactical strike against his wife—
instead, focus on what is best for her and the company.

Now hire this

Q. I work in a family-owned business, and the president wants me to hire his niece to work in our marketing department. She is unqualified, and I don't want to hire her. What should I do?
J.K.

When you work in a family business that is starting to sound like a family reunion, the best step is to meet with the president. However, you should do so only if you are absolutely certain that placing his niece in the job is a major mistake. You need to have a complete understanding of her expertise, or lack of it, along with a clear idea of the demands of the position in which she is to be placed.

Your discussion with the owner should focus on the difficulties that arise when a person is placed in the wrong job. Specifically describe the potential problems and because of this mismatch, and then specifically describe the kinds of problems that this mismatch will cause for his niece.

If this is the wrong job for her, it will generate stress, dissatisfaction, failure, and embarrassment—and that will just be on the first day. In a word, it is unfair to do this to her.

You should then make some suggestions that may help his niece, such as a better position for her elsewhere in the company, some classes for her to take, or a more suitable line of work. Let the owner see that you are interested in what is best for her and the company. If he still insists that you hire her, you will have learned something important about your own relationship with him.

Slightly different rules

Q. I work in the same department as the owner's son-in-law. He always comes in late, leaves early, and gets very little done. If I worked the way he does, I'd be fired. Is there anything I can do?
C.N.

Unless you have some kind of plan to marry into this family, your options are rather limited. Nonetheless, you should try to figure out what is really bothering you here. For example, if this son-in-law has no impact on your work, but his mere presence annoys you because of what he symbolizes, the problem is yours. It will be far more productive for you to focus on getting your job done. By focusing on him, you are letting him interfere with your work.

After all, if the owner spent a tremendous amount of money on a statue and placed it in your department, you might think that it is a big waste, but you do not have to look at it. In your present situation, the owner has put a different kind expensive statue in your department, since this one comes in late and leaves early. In a word, if the son-in-law has as little to do with your work as a statue, that is how he should be viewed.

However, if his work or lack of it is interfering with yours, the first thing to do is meet with him. Tell him that you need his help, and then show him what he needs to do and when he needs to do it.

If he is as responsive as a statue, you should then approach your supervisor. Be sure to pay careful attention—his or her reaction will give you a glimpse into the future.

The supervisor's wife

Q. Our supervisor's wife works in the same office, but in a different department. She constantly looks over our shoulders and tries to control our department. If you disagree with her, she will not talk to you for weeks. Our supervisor loves his wife very much, but we do not. What's your prescription?
N.W.

When a supervisor's wife is a headache, there are a number of prescriptions that may relieve the pain. It is tempting to simply state that as long as she will not talk to you for weeks when you disagree with her, perhaps you and your associates should disagree with her on a regular basis.

A more serious step is for you and your associates to meet with the supervisor's wife in private and express your concerns to her. Describe the specific actions that are creating difficulties for you, let her know in a polite yet businesslike way that you want them to stop, and then tell her that you hope you do not have to go any further with this matter.

If she still insists on playing her control cards, you should meet with your supervisor. Tell him that you are unsure about the way to handle a situation that is interfering with operations in the department, and you would like his help. Then focus your comments on his wife's specific behaviors, and not on her as a person.

If your supervisor either does not or cannot take action, you should consider approaching the next level of management. Your supervisor may love his wife very much, but senior management may not be as enamored with her.

Flounder with the founder

Q. I've been the marketing director for the past 10 years in a family-owned business that is still run by the 85-year-old founder. I find that he is threatened by me and tries to sabotage my success by withholding information, telling other people not to involve me, and manipulating things that I bring in so that he doesn't have to pay me. I'm considering several actions, but I'm not sure what to do.
G.H.

Threats, sabotage, and manipulation are hardly the hallmarks of a successful working relationship. Whether you have been with the company for 10 years or 10 minutes, and whether the founder is 85 or 25, this is a development that calls for direct communication between the two of you.

You should take a careful look at your own performance just to see if there have been any recent changes that may be sending the wrong message. It will also be helpful to look at the situation from the founder's perspective. Like many entrepreneurs, he may be having difficulty letting go of the reins, and this may be compounded by factors related to his age.

In meeting with him, tell him that you have enjoyed working with him and the company over the years, but you are concerned about your working relationship with him. Then let him talk. Along the way, you can mention the costs associated with excluding you from any key processes, along with the benefits associated with keeping you involved, informed, and rewarded. His behavior may be signaling any number of major changes in your job or in the company at large, or it may simply be signaling a temporary communication glitch between the two of you. When you meet with him, it will not take long to figure out which signal is being sent.

Chapter
—18—

Secretarial Mistakes or Mystiques

In any organization, there can be secretaries and assistants who act like jerks, and then there are the jerks who treat their secretaries poorly. Each of these can create any number of problems not only for each other, but for their departments and even the organization at large.

Secretaries can play a crucial role in helping to keep an organization organized, and they can also make crucial errors that keep an organization from ever being organized. Some secretaries glean bits of power from the individuals for whom they work, and they then flex excessively when dealing with just about everyone else. Other secretaries can be overly zealous in protecting their bosses, overly critical in correcting all forms of communication by the rest of the staff, or just plain overly officious.

On the other hand are the managers who are totally clueless when it comes to dealing productively with their secretaries. They do not sense that they are acting like jerks when they ask their secretaries to type their child's school report, or treat the secretaries so harshly that they last for a month or two and then leave.

Problems with secretaries or problems with those who have secretaries tend to be very apparent, and, fortunately, so are the strategies to deal with them.

Beyond the call of duty

Q. Do you think it's right for a boss to ask his secretary to type his daughter's term paper? Some of my friends said that as long as the boss is paying her, what she does with her time is his decision, not hers. What do you think?
S.P.

The daughter's term paper may as well be entitled, "How Dad Managed to Spoil Me." The fact is that the boss does not understand that secretarial assignments need to be based on job-related responsibilities that should have been clearly identified when the individual first accepted the position.

What if this boss now decides that the secretary is to mow his lawn, paint his house, or wash his dog? Although it is understood that a boss plays a major role in establishing assignments and priorities for a secretary, words like autonomy, respect, professionalism, and trust need to be part of the equation.

If the secretary does not want to do this kind of work, she should meet with the boss and honestly spell out her concerns. This meeting is not some sort of an adamant or hostile refusal, but rather a professional-to-professional discussion in which the secretary can indicate that such work is an interruption, an underutilization of her skills, and a waste of money. The secretary can also present an option—perhaps after work, on an hourly basis, she or one of the other members of the support staff can help out. If the boss is any kind of manager, he will understand and respect what the secretary is saying.

As an aside, the term paper was assigned to the boss's daughter. She should at least do some of the typing herself, and then the boss should spend time helping her type the rest. What a concept!

Turnover and over and over

Q. A professional staff member in our firm has gone through five secretaries in the past two years—three of them quit, and he fired the other two. He is very skilled in his work, but the turnover is getting ridiculous. What's the best way to deal with him?
G.T.

The turnover may be due to this professional's style, or his lack of same, but it may also be caused by any number of other factors, such as questionable hiring practices, unfair workload or scheduling assignments, inhospitable working conditions—the list can be endless, and the issues may have nothing to do with the departing employee's boss. After all, there have certainly been situations where long-term secretaries have forced newer secretaries out.

This means that the first step is to do a little data gathering and try to find the real reasons for the excessive departures among employees who work for this individual. If there is any exit interview data, it should be reviewed carefully. It will also be helpful not only to meet with the professional in question, but to meet with the other members of the professional staff and with the support staff to learn their opinions and suggestions regarding this situation.

If all of the data indicate that your firm is in good organizational health, then it is time to deal more directly with the professional. It is not uncommon to find people in management who have strong technical and professional skills, while being totally clueless when it comes to managing others. If the professional in your firm wants to have any chance at controlling turnover, the short-term step is for him to increase the amount of two-way communication that he has with his secretary, and for him to place major emphasis on treating his secretary with more respect, fairness, and trust. The long-term step is for him to enroll in some formal classes in management.

The total cost of replacing an employee is generally estimated to be a year's salary for the position in question. This is something to keep in mind when determining raises and bonuses for this professional staff member. He needs to clearly understand that if he expects to advance, grow, and reap the rewards associated with success in your firm, he needs a complete turnaround in turnover.

Taking notes or taking over?

Q. I was at a meeting that was run by one of the senior managers in our company. His new secretary attended and was supposed to take notes, but she made more comments and asked more questions than most of us. Does this sound right to you?
E.S.

The first question to answer is whether this secretary's participation in the management meeting is a problem, or whether you have a problem with a secretary participating in a management meeting. On the surface, there is absolutely nothing wrong with a secretary participating in a management meeting. In fact, the argument can be made that this is part of effective management.

The secretary's performance in the meeting should be judged by the same criteria that you would apply to all others in attendance. If anyone at the meeting goes into a hyper-verbal mode, then there can be real questions about having that person present, regardless of title.

There is also a need to apply a standard of reasonableness to this whole matter by taking a careful look at the secretary's questions and comments. On the one hand, she is new and may just be stumbling through the early hoops. With some patience, support, guidance, and encouragement from the senior manager and from the management team, she may develop into a highly effective team member. At the same time, if any reasonable person could conclude that her behavior seems to indicate that she is permanently out to lunch, then it's time to discuss the situation with the senior manager.

Your approach with the manager should be to focus on the secretary's specific actions that you believe have undermined the

effectiveness and productivity of the meetings and the management team. It is not your job to establish plans and objectives for
your manager's secretary, but you can provide your manager with
some valuable performance data that he can use in helping this
employee succeed. Your comments can pinpoint some areas where
the secretary's skill mix and knowledge base may need some work,
and they can also help identify some specific behaviors that may
need some adjustment. By taking this approach, it will not take
long to see if she really belongs at the management meetings.

Grammatically speaking

Q. Our secretary is a real stickler for grammar, and she does a good
job cleaning up our writing. The problem is that she corrects us in
our general conversations, and this is both annoying and embar-
rassing. We've talked to her about it, but nothing has changed.
What should we do now?
C.T.

When you have a secretary who corrects you in your general
conversations, this means that you need to correct her in a specific
conversation. She obviously has some real strengths in terms of her
language skills, but when strengths are pushed to an extreme, they
can become weaknesses. Although it is generally easy for people to
see their strengths, they may need a little extra push to see their
weaknesses.

Your secretary's tendency to correct you and your associates
in public is not motivated so much by her desire to hear perfect
linguistics as it is by a desire to hear herself. For any number of
reasons, she has a need to place herself above each of you. After all,
if she were concerned solely with your language, she could talk to
you in private.

Her actions clearly call for a sit-down meeting. In this meeting,
it will be important to indicate that you and your associates appreciate feedback on all kinds of issues from the employees, while
emphasizing that no one appreciates being corrected in public.
However, if your approach is to simply tell her to stop correcting

you and your associates in front of others, you are treating a symptom rather than a cause.

Her behavior is typical of people at many job levels who feel that they have not achieved all that they wanted or expected out of their careers. Because she is not above you in title, her behavior allows her to have the final word or words.

This means that in addition to approaching her with feedback and possible discipline, it makes sense to approach her with coaching, as well. Because she has strong language skills and interests, you should consider encouraging her to not only take some writing classes, but also to teach some classes or provide some private tutoring. There are numerous opportunities in these arenas, and she would feel far better about herself and her career by pursuing them. And, she would then sense far less of a need to impose her words of wisdom on you and your associates.

Editorial excesses

Q. In my new job, one of my responsibilities is to write various reports. I am having a problem with the administrative assistant who works for my manager. She edits my reports and diminishes their quality. How do I deal with this?
A.T.

There typically is little joy in seeing someone armed with a red felt-tipped marker hovering over your written words. It is only natural to believe that your thoughts are so perfectly expressed that the removal of even a comma is tantamount to literary desecration. However, the administrative assistant may have a point.

This means that the first step is to look carefully at your original writing and at the edited version, and then make an honest determination as to which is better. While doing so, remember that you have invested both time and ego in your report, and most people are not particularly receptive to negative feedback on any of their creations.

If you find that you still firmly believe that your report has suffered as a result of her aggressive editing, the next step is to meet with her and discuss your concerns. Bring in your original documents and the edited versions, and go over each of the changes with her. You will need to be able to provide clear and compelling reasons that prove that the changes have somehow diminished your report.

If she is not convinced of the value of your words, your next meeting should be with your manager. Be prepared again to go over your concerns on this matter, and try to obtain a clarification as to the administrative assistant's specific function and responsibility relative to your work. For example, because you are the one who is writing the reports, does she actually have the final voice, or is her role more consultative or advisory?

Whatever the outcome, it will be helpful for you to maintain open lines of communication with her. Whether or not she has final authority, and whether or not she is the best editor in the world, she has some involvement in your work. As a result, you need a clear understanding of her expectations, and she needs a clear understanding of yours. Editorially speaking, things will be better if you work with each other rather than against each other.

Access denied

Q. I am a department manager, and I report to the general manager. His assistant thinks her job is to protect him from everyone. There are many managers like myself who need more access to him. How do we get it?
T.C.

The first question is why she thinks her job is to be the protector. On the one hand, she may have a huge appetite for power. If this is the case, she is in a perfect position to flex. In fact, there are cases of people in this type of position who have actually amassed more power than the people whom they are supposed to protect.

Or she may be exerting this power because your general manager expects her to be a human shield. The typical rationale behind this approach is that if someone really has something important to say to the general manager, he or she will figure out a way to do so.

You and your fellow managers need to meet with the general manager and clear the air. However, you have to get by the gatekeeper in order to do so.

If she either ignores your request for a meeting or agrees to schedule it for sometime in the next millennium, you will need to set the meeting yourself. To do so, you will have to catch the general manager when the sentry is away from her post, such as early in the morning or late in the day. There may also be a way to contact him directly by telephone or e-mail.

When you finally have your meeting, the focus should be on the issue of accessibility. To the extent that his assistant is discussed, it should only be in terms of the responsibilities of her position, and not in terms of her personality. Let the general manager know about any work-related problems that have developed as a result of the lack of access to him, and then present some thoughts as to how to correct things.

For example, it may be worthwhile for the general manager to hold a short stand-up meeting every day where all of you can briefly discuss any key issues, developments, or problems. After all, effective managers spend large amounts of time communicating with the troops and, importantly, effective assistants spend large amounts of time helping them do so.

Lack of support

Q. As the newest and youngest member of the professional staff in a relatively small firm, I am treated as a child by one of the secretaries. She shakes her head, rolls her eyes, and gives a breath of exasperation whenever I ask her to do something. I spoke with her about this, but I don't think she heard a word I said. We don't have an office manager, and I am reluctant to approach any of the professionals about something I should be able to handle myself. What do you suggest?
T.C.

There is an irony in your situation because the only childlike behavior is the secretary's. Your first step was the correct one. When there is a problem with a fellow employee, the best initial action is to visit the source.

In your meeting with her, did she indicate that any of your behaviors are upsetting to her? And, if so, was there any validity to her comments? If you have made some adjustments as a result of this discussion, such as trying to get tight deadline material to her earlier in the day, be sure to let her know that you did this in response to her concerns.

However, if you have made some reasonable accommodations to her needs, but her eyes just keep on rolling, or if there was absolutely no need for such accommodations, then it is time for you to roll on to the office of whoever hires and evaluates the support staff. Give this person specific information regarding the problems and the subsequent actions you have taken, and then ask for his or her suggestions as to what to do next.

Chapter
—19—

Environ-Mental Impacts

The work environment can have a significantly positive or negative impact on employee attitudes, satisfaction, and performance, although it is widely understood that elaborate working conditions will not automatically lead to increased productivity. Nonetheless, if employees have a well-designed, functional, and well-equipped environment, it is far easier for them to focus attention on their jobs, rather than on such is-sues as noise, odors, or the lack of space.

In this regard, it is remarkable what jerks can do to disrupt or destroy the work environment and the performance of employees in it. Environmental problems can attack any of the senses—cramped work areas force people to bump into each other, noisy settings result in auditory assault, smelly settings generate instant nausea, and visually distracting settings practically ignite the retinas.

The special steps that jerks can take to ravage a work environment are virtually endless and can include relocating an employee's office when the employee is out, insisting upon sitting at the employee's desk whenever they meet, wearing questionable attire, and much more. And, the environmental problems can expand beyond the work area and into the parking lot or even the car pool.

There is no question that the work environment has an impact upon all the players. And, there is no question that environmental problems need to be tackled before they start tackling the players.

Cramping your style

Q. I am in middle management and my office is small and cramped. Much of my work involves dealing with the public, and when people come to my office, I am embarrassed. Is it worth talking to my manager about this?
D.T.

If the main problem with the size of your office is that you are embarrassed to work in such a tiny area, you will end up being even more embarrassed by bringing this up with your manager. The discussion will inevitably lead to the point that you should be spending more time thinking about your work and less time thinking about your work environment.

The only reason to approach your manager regarding a matter of this size is if your office is actually interfering with your productivity. For example, if people who visit you can hardly sit down, if there is no room to spread out important papers, or if people are getting injured by trying to angle themselves in and out of your office, then there is a legitimate reason to discuss this issue with your manager.

If there is nothing that either can or should be done with your office, it will be particularly important to remember that the most memorable part of your office is you. If you are embarrassed by the size of your office, your embarrassment is probably being noticed by those who visit you. However, your expertise, competence, and geniality can more than compensate for an office that doubles as a phone booth.

After all, there have been numerous sizable accomplishments emanating from miniscule offices. And, conversely, there have been numerous miniscule accomplishments emanating from sizable offices.

The sardine setup

Q. We work in a small, cramped, and crowded work area, and it is starting to stress all of us out. We can't turn around without bumping into something or someone, and we don't know what to do about it. Can you give us any ideas?
G.P.

When your work area seems to have a lock on the record for the most disgruntled employees per square foot, there are a few steps that you can take...without tripping over each other.

However, there are a couple of pointers to keep in mind before doing so. In the first place, it is a mistake to look at your work environment as a source of satisfaction and motivation. A cramped work area can certainly dissatisfy and de-motivate any employee, but even if a work area is beautiful, spacious, and luxurious, there may be no positive impact on your satisfaction, motivation, or productivity.

This means that one question to ask yourself is whether your work would be satisfying if the obvious aggravation associated with the present working conditions were removed. The real satisfaction from your job is going to come from the achievement, responsibility, and recognition associated with the work itself—and not from the physical amenities of your work area.

If you truly believe that you could be very happy with your job if you were not housed like corporate sardines, then the first step is to meet with your co-workers to discuss specific actions that each of you can take in order to free some space. There may be ways to reconfigure the furniture, remove various barriers, and store or trash any number of items. This approach may provide at least a short-term fix to the problem.

If your group finds that they still need more breathing room, the next step is to develop some cost effective suggestions and present them to management. Let management know that working conditions in your department are undercutting employee attitudes, productivity, and performance. Inform management of the actions that you have already taken to deal with the situation, and then present your cost-effective suggestions for a larger solution.

The response to your suggestions can give you considerable insight into the company's philosophy, mission, and future. It can also give you considerable insight into your own future.

Decorating discord

Q. The company where I work just spent a lot of money refurbishing our department, and now it looks atrocious. The colors clash, the furniture is ugly, and none of us are happy about this. Is there anything we can do now?
C.C.

If your biggest complaint at work is the decor, the first thing to do is consider yourself lucky. With so many elements that can make a job distasteful, one of the easiest to handle is bad taste in decorating.

It sounds like the refurbishing has just been completed. As a result, you have not had enough time to adjust to it. In fact, you and your fellow employees are probably still discovering more outrageous changes daily.

Soon enough, you will be able to place the decor precisely where it belongs—in the background. If you listen, there are probably noises from distant conversations, traffic, or air conditioning right now, but you can ignore them and in essence turn them off. You can do the same thing with the decor, even if it turns you off.

One part of the problem is that your company did not provide adequate two-way communication while implementing changes that affected you and your fellow employees. There is little doubt that if you were given an opportunity to make suggestions during the planning stage, you would be more satisfied with the changes.

Another part of the problem is that people have such different tastes in decorating that it is virtually impossible to find a decor that everyone will like. If you and your co-workers developed a definitive laundry list of decor changes, and management miraculously implemented every single one of them, it would be a matter of time before someone started to play critic.

Although it may be tempting to approach management with swatches and paint chips, you may do little more than demonstrate that you are spending too much time looking at what's on the walls, and too little time looking at what's on your desk.

The only reason to consider approaching management now is if any aspect of the refurbishing is truly interfering with your ability to get your job done. If this is the case, you should be prepared to prove your point and present a cost-effective alternative. This may also help convince management to approach you for more suggestions regarding changes in the future.

Sound decisions

Q. In the facility where I work, there are no fewer than six or seven individual radios or tape players on at the same time and playing different selections of music or talk radio. The level of noise and confusion is irritating and affects my concentration. The manager feels that this is what the majority wants and that is okay. What do you think?
M.B.

What if the majority wanted to bring in their sound-surround systems and twelve-foot speakers? In fact, what if the majority wanted a one-day workweek? This is not the way to make a sound managerial decision.

Unfortunately, your work situation is probably going to get worse. When one employee turns his or her radio or tape player a little louder, a neighboring employee is almost forced to do likewise, and this cycle repeats itself until the work area sounds like a three-ring circus.

There are many voices extolling the virtues of allowing employees to bring radios, tape players, or headsets to work. However, no matter what they bring, there can be problems with employees paying more attention to the music or radio discussions than to their work. In your situation, not only are the employees with the radios or tape players distracted, the noise they generate is distracting those who share the ambient air waves.

It is time for you and any fellow employees who feel the same way about the noise to first meet with your electronically enhanced co-workers. If the decibels continue to ring, your next stop is the manager. His style seems to place major emphasis on being popular. Be specific in describing the costs associated with the present racket, and let him know that these costs will not make him popular with senior management.

Heads up with headsets

Q. Some of my employees have asked me if they can wear stereo headsets while working. I have heard that there can be productivity increases by doing so, but I have my doubts. What do you suggest?

J.F.

If you want to make a sound decision in this area, the first step is to look carefully at the actual jobs within your company. There are numerous positions where headsets would not be appropriate at all. However, if you have many jobs where the employees work mainly on their own and do not require much contact or communication with each other, there is a possibility that allowing them to wear personal stereos may improve productivity.

Unfortunately, highly publicized research studies notwithstanding, you may also find that headsets at work can lead to one big headache. For example, when employees use them, there can be a decrease in communication, camaraderie, and teamwork. In a word, the employees tend to listen to music rather than to each other.

When a person is listening to a personal stereo, he or she is not typically motivated to take it off to ask or answer questions. In fact, when employees are sporting these headsets, their body language often sends a "do not disturb" message, and this can be enough to stifle communication—even if the employee is more than willing to remove the headset and talk.

In jobs that do not call for much interaction, there is still a good deal of informal communication that can help prevent or solve problems and build employee solidarity—personal stereos remove this element from the workplace. In essence, communication can end up being viewed as an intrusion.

The productivity increases in the personal stereo studies may have occurred because the employees played a role in the decision-making that permitted them to use headsets in the first place. Countless studies have found a clear link between employee involvement in decision-making and subsequent increases in productivity.

In addition, the use of personal stereos on the job can raise safety issues, and there is a possibility of damaging an employee's hearing as well. The bottom line is that when you open that personal stereo box at work, you may be opening Pandora's Box, as well.

The nasal assault

Q. I have "fragrance sensitivity," and for the past year I have been trying to have an accommodation at work. I asked one person to refrain from wearing perfume because of my medical problem, and when I made the same request of another person, I got perfume poured on my desk. Management has refused to help me. What should I do?

J.O.

This situation stinks in more ways than one. Management obviously does not understand that your fragrance sensitivity is a disability, a fact that points to their own insensitivity and inability. Not only have they failed to take any productive action regarding your condition, they have failed to do anything in response to the harassment by at least one of your co-workers.

You made the right move by first going directly to the perfumed co-workers. Although it is not entirely reasonable to expect these individuals to refrain from wearing any perfume, they can be asked if they can cut back the dosage. And, if the perfume is particularly pungent, perhaps there are other employees who would be willing to join you.

It may be also helpful for you to try to educate management about this disability and the meaning of reasonable accommodation. For example, management may want to look at office location, barriers, and ventilation, as well as to consider developing and enforcing policies that spell out the company's commitment to maintaining a hospitable and refreshing atmosphere for all employees.

Extremely casual attire

Q. I am a department manager in an organization that allows the employees to "dress down" on Fridays. There is no written policy in this area, and many employees are wearing clothes that are inappropriate for work. Lately some of our customers have made comments. How do I deal with this?
H.D.

When employees are told that they can "dress down," and the guidelines are vague at best, the employees will dress down...in many cases, way down. And further, the attire will continue its descent unless some action is taken.

Programs that allow the employees to dress comfortably for work can be very helpful in improving morale, satisfaction, and even productivity. It is not critical to have a written policy in this area, but it is essential to have widely shared agreement as to what is and is not appropriate. The best way to reach this understanding is through direct communication.

The first step is to openly and honestly tell the employees that the current level of attire on Fridays has dipped into the unacceptable range, to the point that customers are commenting about it. Give them specific information regarding the kinds of attire that have generated complaints or other work-related problems, as well as a clearer picture of the kinds of attire that are acceptable. Let the employees know that you view them as adults and expect them to make reasonable individual decisions as to what they should be wearing to work on the free-dress days.

In the event that some employees still do not get the message, the next step is to develop a more formalized standard. You could do this on your own, but it will be more effective to form a task force of key employees to suggest some guidelines. By having employee involvement at this stage of the process, you increase the likelihood of having a quality program that is actually followed.

Although not a major issue, one change that should be considered is the name of the program. The term, "dress down," can send a psychological message that attire is expected to sink to greater and greater depths—in fact, it is almost a subtle directive to do so.

As a result, it will make more sense to use words like "casual" or "comfortable" in referring to attire for the special days.

In the dog house

Q. I work for a woman who brings her dog to work. I knew ahead of time that she did this, but I did not know that the dog smells, makes a mess, and is always in the way. A customer recently asked if the office is a kennel. Do you have any suggestions?
M.F.

The issue that you raise is a mixed bag, specifically in this case, a mixed doggy bag. On the one hand, there is a growing body of literature indicating that the presence of pets at work can have many benefits, ranging from increased satisfaction and morale, to reduced blood pressure and stress.

At the same time, the presence of a pet that is untrained, noisy, or smelly can wreak havoc in a company. In such situations, it is not uncommon to find that pets can destroy morale, not to mention furniture.

Because it sounds like your company pet is making people petulant, the best step is to meet with the owner. It is important for her to see specific examples of the problems that her dog is causing. There may be some compromises that can work here, such as keeping the dog in a more limited area, bringing the dog to work on an intermittent basis, checking the dog's grooming, and the like.

It is then up to the owner of the company to listen to your comments or bury them. If she is willing to let the company go to the dogs, it may be time for you to take a walk.

The chair man

Q. Every time my manager meets with me in my office, he has to sit in my chair behind my desk. I don't like this, but if I say anything, I am sure he will get upset or think I have a problem. Should I just let it go?
C.S.

The fact that your manager has to sit in your chair in your office can be interpreted in countless ways. It can be a power play, a need to hide behind a protective barrier, an inability to read upside down (think about that), or perhaps he just likes your chair.

The real problem is that you are certain he will get upset if you mention this issue to him. For you to have a productive working relationship with your manager, you need the freedom to openly discuss virtually any work-related issue. If you fear some kind of retribution for discussing a relatively minor matter, what happens when a serious problem arises?

At this point, one approach is to tell your manager that it makes more sense for you to sit behind your desk when the two of you meet in your office. Put your comments in the context of making these meetings more productive. For example, tell him that it will be easier for you to access needed information during these meetings if you are at your desk. If this does not work, try suggesting that you meet in his office. This incident certainly makes it easier to see why King Arthur opted for the round table.

On the phone again

Q. Whenever I go to lunch with my manager, he brings his cellular phone. I'd like to talk business with him during the meal, but I can hardly complete a sentence or two before his phone rings, and then he's back on it. What do you suggest?
N.H.

Here's some food for thought: Your manager has made it known that he is accessible by phone throughout the day. There is nothing inherently wrong with this, and, in fact, it may be exactly what your business requires. There does not appear to be any incentive for him to change, and it could easily be argued that he should not even think about doing so.

This means that you have a number of options. For example, if you really need to spend some quality time with him, schedule a meeting.

In terms of lunches that are disconnected and dissatisfying, you can skip them altogether, or eat by yourself or with someone else.

Another option is for you to bring along some work or a newspaper so that you have something to do while he is chatting away. An additional option is for you to invite some of your associates to join the two of you for lunch. At least you could talk business with them, unless their phones ring.

If it is somehow required that you must have lunch with your manager, the final option is for you to bring your own phone. Perhaps you could use it to call your manager and finally talk some business with him during the meal!

A moving experience

Q. When I returned from a short vacation, I found that my office had been moved from one part of the building to another. I never had been told about this, and no one else's office was moved. I am furious. I told my manager and he said that it just needed to be done. Does this sound right to you?
C.B.

There can be some good reasons for management to move an employee's office when the employee is not present, but most are related to disasters such as earthquakes, fires, or monsoons. When management unilaterally moves an employee's office under most other circumstances, it simply causes a disaster.

Even if your manager is somehow correct and your office just needed to be moved, whatever that means, there still should have been communication with you regarding this prospect.

Looking at the bigger picture, you need to ask yourself if this kind of treatment is typical of the way that your company is run. If this is some sort of an aberration, it will be important for senior management to understand your dissatisfaction with the process, as well as your desire to be directly involved in any such decisions in the future.

At the same time, if this moving experience is typical of the way that things are done in your company, you need to decide if you can live with this managerial style, or if it is time for you to move.

Maybe time to jump out of the pool

Q. I car-pool to work every day with three of my co-workers. Lately we have been listening to a radio program that I think is stupid and gross. I do not like starting the day this way, but everyone else seems to be enjoying it. How do I deal with this?
S.W.

When you feel that things are not going swimmingly in this pool, the first place to turn is toward your fellow riders. Because you indicated that they seem to enjoy the radio program, it sounds like you have not directly asked them their opinion, nor have you voiced your concern. Hence, that is the first order of business.

If they all enjoy the program, your next step is to see if there can be any flexibility or courtesy here. For example, if you are really upset by the program, they may forego it. Or, with four people in the car pool, another option may be to let each person select a station on a given day, with the driver getting a bonus day.

If this approach does not work, there are things you can do instead of listening, such as bringing your own headset and listening to something else. Although this is not the most sociable thing to do, you would only resort to this if your car-pool mates were not being particularly sociable in the first place.

It is also important to remember that car pools come and go. If you are not happy with this one, instead of trying to change stations, it may make more sense to change car pools.

A parking lot, but not a lot of parking

Q. The office where I work has more employees than there are spaces in the employee lot. There is a parking lot for guests and customers, but the employees are not permitted to use it, even though there is ample space. Employees without a parking spot must park their vehicles on the street. Do you have any suggestions?
C.J.

It can be tempting to walk into your manager's office, park yourself at his or her desk, and complain about the number of parking spaces. However, your manager may be equally tempted to respond with, "When we can manufacture more parking spaces, we'll call you."

The best strategy is to approach management with some creative ideas, and you do not need to have them in mind before the meeting. Rather, consider telling the manager that the shortage of employee parking spaces is creating dissatisfaction, and you and some of your co-workers would like to research the problem and develop some cost-effective suggestions.

In the process, you and your associates may find that more parking spaces can be generated by restriping, or maybe there is a way to stack the parking. Perhaps there is never a time when the customer lot is more than 60-percent full. What about more incentives or flexibility for those employees who car-pool or use public transportation? Other approaches await you as well.

The real message is that in parking lots and in virtually any other aspect of work, employee input can do lots of good.

Supplies and demands

Q. Our department has goals, but we have so many problems with supplies and equipment that we can't meet them. We've talked to our manager about this, but all he says is, "Do your best." What do we do now?
D.O.

Some companies have real goals, while others have fool's goals. Unfortunately, it sounds like yours is in the latter category.

On the surface, fool's goals can shine—they may have measurable standards, perhaps some priorities, and maybe even benchmarks and deadlines. The problem is that there is no topside commitment or support associated with meeting them, and the company has not provided the employees with adequate resources to do so.

By approaching your manager, you have already taken the best first step. However, your manager's "do your best" response is shorthand for, "Sorry, it's not my committee."

Because work is more satisfying and rewarding when there are achievable goals, and, many employees enjoy the challenge of solving problems that are interfering with their work, you should make this your committee. Tell your manager that you are still concerned about the supply and equipment problem, and that you and some of your fellow employees would like to try to come up with some cost-effective suggestions to solve it.

Your manager may respond with reservations regarding the amount of time that this may take, so you will need to indicate that your formal job responsibilities will remain as the top priority, while this project will be approached as an additional commitment.

It may help to emphasize the fact that if you and your co-workers can find cost-effective solutions to the problem, everybody will win: the company, your department, your manager, and you. However, this can only happen if you get a commitment from your manager to give your findings and recommendations serious consideration.

At this point, the time will have arrived for you and your fellow employees to develop and follow a plan to figure out which supply and equipment issues ail the company and how they can be cured.

The less obvious benefit associated with this approach is that you will be acting like a manager, and your skills in doing so could play a role in the promotion process. When it comes to handling projects beyond your assigned range of responsibilities, it's nice to show the topsiders that you can manage very well.

In
Conclusion

The best way to deal with jerks at work is to make sure that you have a clear understanding of their questionable behaviors, and then tailor your response to fit the particular person and situation. It is my hope that this book has offered you that understanding and has presented you with enough real-life situations to give you plenty of exercise in jerk-negotiation skills. Some cases will call for swift, direct, and assertive action, while others will call for more subtlety, patience, and persuasion.

But let's not lose sight of another perspective—that you, yourself, might from time to time be responsible for jerk-like behavior! Of course, now that you've read this book, you'll be particularly sensitive to signs of such behavior and take steps to eliminate it.

Many people learn how to become jerks at work by copying their managers and fellow employees. This means that the less we act like jerks, the less likely our associates will do so. There are some key pointers that anyone at any job level should keep in mind in order to be a positive role model, rather than a model jerk:

- Treat people with respect and trust.
- Listen to what others have to say.
- Be fair and honest.
- Set positive expectations.
- Recognize the value of diversity.
- Keep the lines of communication open.

- Be a team player.
- Keep furthering your education.
- Establish realistic plans and goals.
- Look for solutions, not just problems.
- Try to understand others as individuals.
- Give thanks and recognition when due.
- Keep quality and service in clear focus.
- Encourage innovative and creative thinking.
- And, *most importantly*, remember that only a jerk ignores the Golden Rule.

It is my hope that this book will arm you with the knowledge and sensitivity to combat jerk behavior in your employers, co-worker, employees—and, most importantly, in yourself.

If you still find that you need an extra edge in dealing with jerks at work, or if you have questions pertaining to other people-related issues and problems on the job, you can contact me at LloydOnJob@aol.com, or P.O. Box 260057, Encino, CA 91426.

Index

Absence,
  from work place, 61-62
  of manager, 95, 97-98,
  101-102
Accidents, attributed to
  manager, 26-27
Advice, bad, 63
Age discrimination,
  interviewing, 14
Appointments, being late for,
  45
Arrogance, employee, 82
Assignments, unpleasant,
  124
Attendance, poor, 95
Attire, casual, 242
Attitude, negative, 63-64,
  131-132
Awards, displaying of, 25

Bad attitude, 63-64, 131-132
Badgering, employees,
  85-86
Blamestorming, 79
Blaming, 48, 70-71
Borrowers, 145

Boss,
  conflict with, 28-29
  access to, 231-232
  going around supervisors,
  104, 106, 107-108
  who meddle, 111-112
Bragging, 72-72
Brush-off, from manager,
  92-93

Car pools, 246
Casual days, 242
Certificates, displaying of, 25
Cliques, 37-38, 75-76, 76-77,
  161-162
Co-workers, 139-150
Commissions, 181
Company loyalty, 31-32
Complainers, 170
Computer changes, 163
Confidence, broken, 144
Conflicts, employee, 65-79
Contests, employee, 206-207
Corporate cultures, 36
Credit, stealing, 54, 147-148
Crisis management, 57

Criticism,
  at meetings, 184
  from manager, 128, 129, 130
  of employees, 49
Cube farm, 79
Customers, demanding, 155

Decision-making, 105-106,
Decor, of office, 238
Degrees,
  displaying of, 25
  insecurity about, 174
Discipline, of employees,
  115-116
Discrimination, sexual, 120
Disruptions, in meetings,
  186-187
Dress down days, 242

Editing, employee work,
  230-231
Education, employee, 200-201
Employee conflicts, 65-79
Employee evaluations, 33
Employee gifts, 211-212
Employee referrals, 142, 210
Employee suggestions, 212
Employees,
  conflict with, 28-29
  feuding, 152, 153, 158
  training, 195-204
  uncooperative, 24-25, 27-28,
  30-31
  unproductive, 73, 74
Employer screening, 12
Evaluations, 33, 138
Exceptions, to rules, 119-120

Exit interview, 160
Extroverts, 96-97
Eye contact, during
  interview, 16

Fair treatment, 121-122
Family businesses, 215-224
Favoritism, 120-121, 123,
  125, 126
Feedback, conflicts, 127-138
Feuding, among employees,
  152, 153, 158-159
Firing employees, 110-111
First impressions, 23
Flirting, 177-178
Franklin, Benjamin, 64
Friendly insults, 174-175

Gifts, to employees,
  211-212

Happy hour, 75-76
Harassment, 158
Headquarters, offsite, 94
Headsets, use of, 240-241
Hiring mistake, 15, 69

Incentive program, 210-211,
  213
Industrial Revolution, 30
Inequitable pay, 206
Insubordination, 25
Insults, 128, 175-176, 182
Internal sales, 82
Internet, employer screening,
  12
Interruptions, 42

Interview,
  age discrimination, 14
  bad, 20, 22
  exit, 160
  eye contact, 16
  internal positions, 21
  multiple interviewers, 18
  personal questions, 13-14
  personal references, 17
  pre-employment tests, 13
  salary information, 19
  screening employer, 12
  with boss, 106
Introverts, 96-97

Jealous employees, 125

Lay-offs, interviews, 19
Leader, among employees, 25,
  36-37, 130
Lenient management, 34
Listening, 60-61
Long-term employees, 24
Loyalty, to company, 31-32

Management styles, 34
Manager,
  aligned with employees,
    31-32
  conflicts, 103-116
  different styles, 34
  in title only, 105
  new job, 24, 33
Manners, 133
Marginal, employees, 87
Meddling, bosses,
  111-112

Meetings, 183-193
  boring, 185
  disruptions, 186-187
  role of secretary, 228
  unprepared at, 191
Memos, 62
Mentor, 200
Mission statements, 193
Moodiness, in managers, 41
Motivational programs, 90
Murphy's Corollary, 144
Murphy's Law, 144
Music, in the office, 239-240

Negative attitude, 131-132
New hires, intimidated by
  employees, 112-113
New job, 23-38
Nicknames, use of, 53
Nitpicking, 122-123
Noisy employees, 67

Office
  decor, 238
  size of, 236, 237
  supplies, 247-248
Offsite, headquarters, 94
Open-door policies, 43,
  100-101
Overanalyzing, employees,
  84-85
Overreactions, 157
Oversupervision, 47

Paperwork, complaints, 169
Parking, 246-247
Parties, company, 208

Pay, inequitable, 206
Perfectionists, 46
Perfume, in the office, 241
Personal phone calls,
74-75
Personal questions, 13-14
Personal references,
interview, 17
Personality tests, 137,
203-204
Personality types, training
program, 197-198,
203-204
Petitions, 143
Pets, at work, 243
Phone calls,
during meetings, 244-245
personal, 74-75
Political disagreements, 156
Pre-employment, 11-22
tests, 13
Problem people, 37
Productivity, 29-30
Promotion, 30, 104, 140
Psychologist, employees as,
69
Public humiliation, by
manager, 60

Quality improvement, 190
Questionnaires, 171

Radios, in the office, 239-240
Rate buster, 30
Reduced responsibilities,
99-100
References, interview, 17

Referrals, employee, 142, 210
Research, 84
Responsibilities, reduced, 164

Sabotage, by employees, 113
Salaries,
confidentiality, 207-208
inequitable, 206
revealing, 209
Salary information,
interviews, 19
Secret Pals, 146
Secretarial conflicts, 225-233
Secretaries,
editing employees, 230-231
meetings, 228
turnover, 227
Sick, working while, 66
Socializing, employees, 75-76
Staffing, complaints, 168
Stress interviews, 18
Suggestions,
employee, 88, 212
from bosses, 104
Superstitious, employees,
86-87
Supplies, office, 247-248

Talkative, manager, 58
Tantrums, 49, 83, 157
Teasing, from employees,
69-70
Telephone calls,
during meetings, 244-245
personal, 74-75
Termination, of employees,
110-111

Testing, pre-employment, 13
Threes, working in, 149-150
Top Gun, 53
Trainers, 198-199
Training program,
  boring, 197
  disappointments, 196
  personality types, 197-198,
  203-204
Training, 195-204
Turnover, employee, 12, 112,
  227

Uncooperative employees,
  24-25, 27-28, 30-31
Undermining, from bosses,
  104
Unpleasant assignments, 124
Unproductive, employees, 73,
  74

Vacations, 78-79
Vocabulary, company, 79

Work environment, 235-248